I'LL WAIT FOR YOU MY DARLING

To Amber
with love

[signature]

Karl Kern

I'll Wait For You My Darling

Against all the rules, a World War II prisoner
and a beautiful English girl meet and fall in love.
Despite obstacles and enforced separations they are eventually
united.

Adelante Books

FIRST EDITION

Published by
Adelante Books, a division of
Adelante Industries LLC
PO Box 710952
Santee, CA 92072-0952
USA

www.adelante-books.com

Printed in the United States of America

ISBN 1-931856-01-X

Cover design by Christina Kern/Wolfgang Black

I dedicate this book to
my dear wife who was my life's partner for 47 years,
also to my son Peter and my granddaughter Christina.

ACKNOWLEDGEMENTS

Cousin Lorna is still living in England. Cousin Kathy emigrated with her husband to Australia where she died of cancer. Her husband Gordon also passed away there. I have not seen or heard of little George, nor my friend Walter since I last saw them in England at the P.O.W. camps. It is my hope that my friend and companion Struppie lived a long and happy life with his new owner on the farm.

Thank you to my dear friend Jennifer Van Westrum who, when reading some of my letters while I was writing this book, came up with the title "I'll wait for you my Darling."

A special thanks to my friend Collin Whatmuff, the artist who designed the picture on the back cover. Both he and his dear wife Barbara have been long time friends of ours since we lived in England.

Thank you also to my friends who helped me to get started by putting all my handwritten pages on the computer at the very early stages of this book. They are: Jeany Deake, My nephew David Maeding, and my good friends Benny Hinnen and Peter Antoniak.

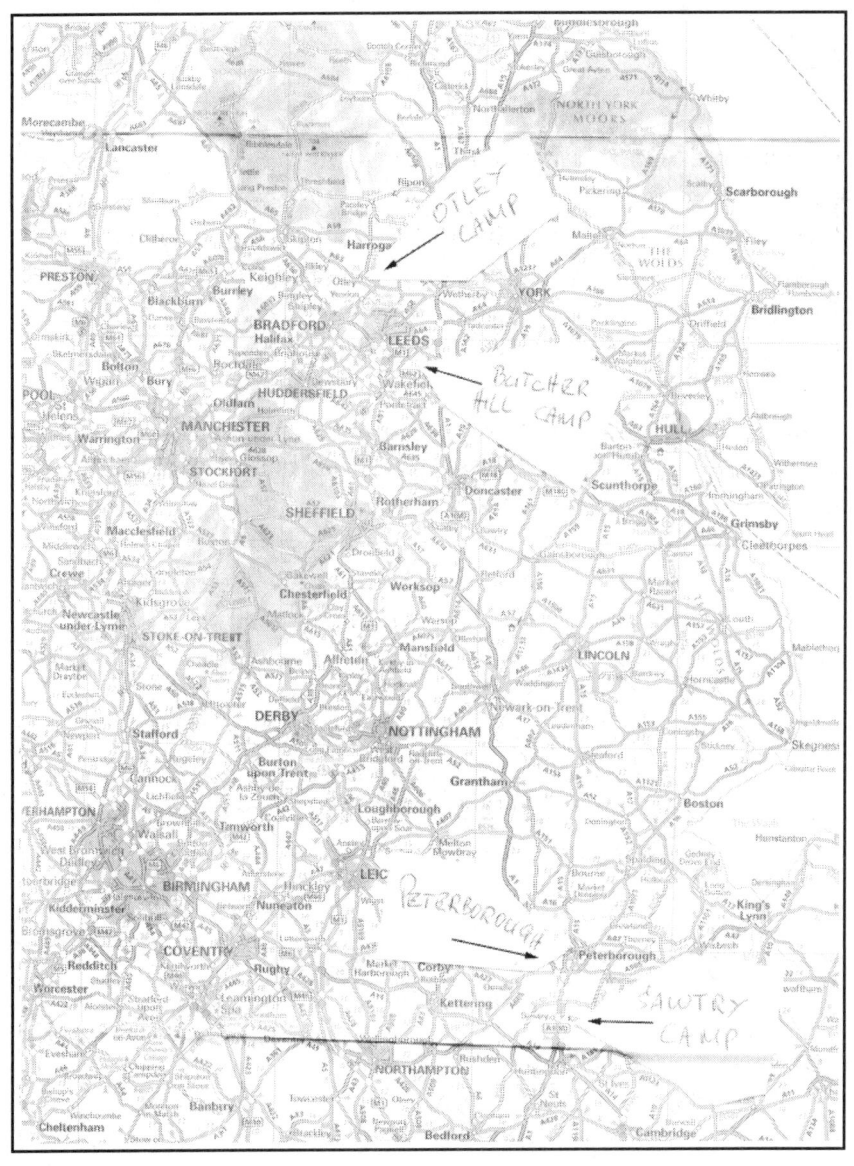

The location of the POW camps in England

Eningen, Germany

1

I grew up in a small village called Eningen-unter-Achalm, in the southern German state of Wuerttemberg. The Second World War began and Hitler's armies set out to conquer the world. My parents were very religious people. I never heard them talk politics but I knew that they were not happy with the things that were going on. Most of the friends and neighbors of my age, and those I had gone to school with, joined the Hitler Youth, but my parents did not want me to be part of it.

On completion of grade school, when I was just fourteen years old, I decided that I wanted to be a tool and die maker. It was recognized as a very respectable profession and I was told that according to my grades and aptitudes I would be suitable for it. I was advised to apply for an apprenticeship with a company called Wafios, short for Wagner, Ficker and Schmied. The company was located in Reutlingen, about three miles from where we lived.

I applied and was invited to take an aptitude test as well as a test in arithmetic, science and a few other subjects. About a week later I was told that I had passed all the tests and that I should report to the company to fill out the necessary forms before being accepted. One of the questions on the form was *'Are you a member of the Hitler Youth?'* This I had to answer with a no.

A few days later I received a note from the company telling me that unless I joined the Hitler Youth movement I could not be accepted for an apprenticeship. I was very upset and begged my father to let me join for the sake of my career. He promised to think it over.

I learned from my friends that young people were needed to join the music band in another of Hitler's movements, for a younger age group, called 'Jung Volk' which was similar to the Boy Scouts. My father agreed that I could join them and thus I became a member of the band playing the fanfare, which was acceptable to Wafios. After a very intensive training, which included attending college for two full days every week, I successfully completed my apprenticeship after three and a half years.

In 1942 Germany occupied France and many of the boys I had gone to school with were in the German army. My brother Walter was a pilot and training to be a fighter pilot. I was also supposed to be called up to join one of Hitler's armies, but was detained by my company because I was a specialist and therefore someone who was needed to support Hitler's war machine. Being at home, when nearly all my friends were in the military, made me increasingly uncomfortable. I felt as though the mothers, whose boys were in the war, looked at me as if to say, "How come you are still at home?" I did not feel right going to work every day while my school friends were out there defending their country.

I knew that sooner or later I was going to be called up to the military anyway, so I decided to volunteer for the air force. I wanted to be a flyer like my brother and I liked the smart uniform. However I first had to convince my father, who would have to sign my application papers and give his consent. After several days of discussing the matter he finally agreed. I had to pass a very rigorous physical test as well as a day-long test in a classroom, answering questions about history, sociology, metallurgy, science and arithmetic. It reminded me very much of the exams I had to take at the end of my apprenticeship. I passed all the tests and felt very pleased with myself. I imagined coming home on leave wearing a smart air force uniform.

When I was just 18 years old I served my basic training in France. However, it was nothing like I had pictured it to be. Physically, I was in very good condition, which helped me to get through the rigorous training better than many of my fellow volunteers. I had never experienced anything so tough. Three of the boys who served in my unit took their own lives by shooting themselves because they could not stand the stress. The immense heat in the south of France did not help. We were made to run for hours, wearing gas masks, during the hottest time of the day. Over and over again we were shouted at by the trainers, "What, you want to fly and you don't even know how to walk?" Many times I wished I were back at Wafios.

After my basic training, much to my disappointment, I was sent to school to be a radio operator, instead of becoming a pilot. I also learned how to land a plane in case of an emergency. By the time I completed my training the war had taken a turn for the worse.

2

In 1945 I was 20 and a fully trained radio operator in the German Air Force. We flew mainly Junker 88s or Messerschmitt 110s. The enemy had destroyed most of our fuel supplies and consequently we were grounded.

At that point I was given the choice of joining the SS or the paratroopers. I decided to serve in the paratroopers and was again sent on a special course in the city of Stendal, which was known as a paratrooper training center.

After climbing a twenty-foot tower, we were hooked to a steel wire at the top. We then had to slide down it, at a speed equal to that of coming down in a parachute, and at some point we were released and fell to the ground. This way we learned how to fall, wearing full battle gear and without getting hurt. We were also taught how to fold a parachute and how to jump out of an airplane. Often I wondered if I had made the right choice, but I knew that I didn't want to be part of the SS.

By this time I had very mixed feelings about life in general. My young life seemed to have no purpose and there was a senseless war going on, with no end in sight.

Soon afterwards, I was commissioned to join the second paratrooper division. Our unit was dropped behind enemy lines near Nijmegen in the Netherlands, a hot spot on the western front. Our task was to stop the advancement of the American troops until our units had regrouped. This was to be my very first taste of facing an enemy in combat. We called it *'die Feuertaufe'* (the baptism with fire).

I was assigned to be the leader of a group of eight men. One of them was Walter, a seasoned paratrooper who had served for two years in combat on the Russian front. Walter was slightly smaller than me and very stocky. He had keen eyes and a lot of experience in warfare. He was my assistant and also my gunner.

The machine gun he carried was one of Germany's fastest, 250 rounds a second. He told me that it was the best-engineered weapon he had ever come across, except for one thing; the tolerances were too close. It jammed and malfunctioned whenever some dirt or sand got into the mechanism. It was a precision-built weapon, whereas the Russian guns were very ruggedly built. They were a lot slower than ours but, according to Walter, one could trail them through mud and grime and they would still go on shooting.

Even though I was Walter's superior in rank, I learned a lot from him and I was glad that I had him in my group. Whenever we had a chance we would talk together. He would say to me, "Karl, don't stick your neck out, believe me, it isn't worth it." One day he said, "I was a prisoner in Russian hands for a few days."

"You must be kidding me," I said, " So what happened? How did you get away?"

He explained that a Russian soldier was guarding him, four days after his capture. They were near a railroad station, waiting for a train to transport all the prisoners to Siberia. Most German prisoners were taken there.

As they were sitting on an embankment my friend Walter sensed that the German troops were very close. He saw an opportunity to escape if he could distract the guard long enough to get some twenty yards away from him. After that he would have enough cover even if he was shot at. He made his mind up to give it a try and motioned to the guard that he would like a cigarette. The Russian soldiers were not issued cigarettes but they had loose tobacco in one of their trouser pockets. In another pocket they had paper with which to roll the tobacco into a cigarette. The guard put his rifle down beside him and concentrated on making a cigarette for Walter. My friend then jumped to his feet and ran for his life. Moments later he heard shots ring out. Some of them came very close but by then he had good ground cover and he reached the German side safely.

Walter had a very dry humor. Whenever we were huddled together as a group awaiting orders, he would tell us of his experiences in Russia in a joking kind of way.

This time things did not look good. Our troops had suffered heavy casualties, and the enemy had broken through our lines several times. Early one morning the Americans pushed forward through our lines again and I became separated from my company. We were suddenly under fire from very close range.

I threw myself down into what seemed to be a shallow ditch. However it turned out to be full of water. In fact my body was completely submerged. I had to keep my head sideways so that I could breathe. I knew that the American troops were close by so I had no choice but to lie there and wonder how I could get myself out. None of our people were around to help me and I was afraid. This could be the end of me or I could be taken prisoner at any time. There was nothing in the book on how to behave in a situation like this. All I knew was that if I was to be taken prisoner, under no circumstances was I to disclose any of our military positions, nor to which unit I belonged. It was drummed into us that, when interrogated, the only thing we were allowed to say was name, rank, and serial number.

Desperately I tried to come up with a plan to get myself out of this mess. I was getting cold. It was springtime, so the water was freezing and the air was misty. The wind blew from the direction of the enemy troops. Every time I attempted to move I was shot at from two different locations. Consequently, I was forced to lie in the same spot for several hours. The enemy was so close that I could hear them talking. I recognized their voices as American. Since they knew I was there I expected them to come and take me prisoner. However, nothing happened. I wished that they would come and get me out of this hole. Maybe they were not sure themselves what they saw.

One single grenade would have finished me off. I was close enough for them to reach me with one. I thought of my family at home. My brother Walter would have tried his best to rescue me. When we were boys he used to get me out of all sorts of sticky situations. But this was war and who knew where he was. I was alone and helpless.

To judge by the position of the sun it was late afternoon. I hoped that by nightfall I would be able to get away because I could not lie like this for much longer. Every bone in my body was aching. I was tempted to put my hands up into the air and shout, "Schiesst nicht. Ich komme raus." ("Don't shoot. I am coming out.") However I decided against it. Their guns must have been pointed at me. If I suddenly raised my head up someone might pull the trigger.

The minutes felt like hours. Though I had not had anything to eat for almost two days, I did not feel hungry. And anyway, my iron ration, (a small can of dry biscuits) was out of reach. After lying in the icy cold water for almost a day my body was stiff and I was shivering. I had to tell myself that I would be all right once it got dark. Some inner voice told me to hold out and not give up.

As it got dark I tried to move forward. After I had painfully crawled about 10 feet forward, shots rang out again. Since I was now near a large tree the bullets ricocheted above me. I stopped moving and the shooting stopped too. I couldn't figure out what they saw every time I moved. Then I realized that I was carrying a gas mask on my back, and that is what they saw moving above the ditch.

Before long it was completely dark. Luckily the water was a little shallower where I was lying and the ditch was somewhat wider. This enabled me to turn a little sideways and remove my gas mask without being shot at. I also had to leave behind everything I was carrying except for the 30-caliber Luger in my top pocket. The mud that covered me hindered me from doing almost anything.

Everything was now very quiet. The silence around me almost drove me insane. All night I wondered what would happen next. When daylight came I heard the voices again from about fifty yards away.

My body was so numb that I could hardly move any of my limbs and it was becoming increasingly difficult for me to control my thoughts.

The sun came up through the trees to herald the morning and the warm rays felt good on one side of my exposed face. My whole body must have been very exhausted, because I was beginning to doze off occasionally. I had to fight with myself to keep a clear mind. During the past days and weeks I had spent a lot of time in difficult situations, but this was different. All through the day I had nightmares on and off. I tried to assess my situation, but my mind did not function properly.

As night fell again, I made up my mind that I was going to get out of this ditch no matter what happened. To stay in the mud and water would have been suicide. If I were shot at, at least I would have a slim chance of getting away. Besides, I didn't care any more whether I lived or died.

Covered in mud and with frozen limbs, I didn't know how I was even going to stand up, much less to run, but the noises had stopped again so I edged myself inch by inch out over the rim of the ditch. I was still lying on the ground and my heart was pounding furiously. Somehow I managed to get up; then I started moving as best I could in the direction where I thought the German troops were. The mud, which was half frozen to my body, and the pain in my joints made it very difficult for me to put one foot in front of the other.

After I had been going for about 20 minutes I was suddenly shot at with trace ammunition from ahead of me. As I had been trained, I took shelter behind a tree and shouted, "Schiesst nicht. Ich bin Deutscher," ("Don't shoot. I am German.") The shooting stopped. Everything was quiet. Again I shouted, "Don't shoot. I am German." All I could hear was my heartbeat, which gave me the assurance that I was still alive. After a while a voice in German ordered me to put my hands up and come forward. By this time I was on the verge of exhaustion, but I had to make those last 20 yards.

When I got up to the German troops I collapsed. How long I was out I don't know, but after I came round I was given a hot drink and treated like a prisoner, searched and questioned. Then I realized that my dog tag and everything that would identify me was missing. After I had managed to convince them who I was they gave me dry clothes and food. That night, besides having nightmares about being taken prisoner, I slept like a baby. Two days later I was reassigned to my company.

Eibergen, Holland

3

It was a cold, gray morning when the second paratrooper division was ordered to dig in. No one was allowed to leave his position under any circumstances. Days before we had been encircled by the enemy and consequently our food supply was cut off. Shrubs in a densely wooded area camouflaged my part of the unit. We were all hungry, tired and cold. I was assigned to keep communications open with the battalion headquarters and to report new orders to our company lieutenant. Apart from the occasional grenade hits the night was fairly quiet. During a lull in the fighting we were able to collect our dead and the medics could take care of the wounded. The morale of our troops was very low.

At the first sign of twilight I made my way under the cover of two machine guns to the headquarters about a mile away. I was about half way there when I was seen by the enemy and shot at with grenade throwers. The grenades followed me as I ran. Some shots came very close as I was now in an area with very little cover. When I arrived at the headquarters I was told that we were surrounded, this time by a Canadian division. We had orders to withdraw via the only road still open, which was pointed out to me on my map. I was then informed that whatever happened I must deliver the message if we were to make it out. I reached my unit by a different route without being detected. Speed was important because we had to pull back under cover of night.

After returning to my unit I learned that our lieutenant had jumped onto one of the last of our tanks leaving the area, and deserted. I was shocked. How could anyone do such a thing, especially when he was responsible for so many men. Since the lieutenant was no longer there, I reported to the second-in-command and informed him of the order to withdraw. After talking to him about the situation I realized that he had no idea what to do and also that he was a coward. I told him to give orders that everything anyone carried had to be secured so as to make as little noise as possible, and that under no circumstances would anyone be allowed to use a flashlight. Since I was the only one who knew the way out of the surrounded area he asked me to lead the company. Somehow I managed to find the way out without incident and we finally got clear. We were then regrouped as ordered in a wooded area outside the city of Eibergen in Holland.

By now the allied forces were advancing rapidly towards Germany. The morale among our troops was deteriorating visibly. We were not informed about the grave situation we were in, but everyone knew it could not go on much longer. There were inadequate supplies, hardly enough food to go around, and confusion among the leadership. For the last three weeks we had done nothing but huddle in holes, make a stand, retreat and regroup. Casualties were heavy. Sometimes we did not know who our enemies were; the British, Canadian, or American troops.

This time the 8th Canadian tank division was coming towards us. We were inadequately equipped for such a force. There was not one German tank and no air force to support us. I was group leader. I had a few rifles, one antitank gun and one machine gun. Most of my group consisted of young recruits who had been trained how to use a rifle in a three-week boot camp and then assigned to the front lines. My second-in-command, Walter, had more experience in warfare than any of us. Dug in next to me in his hole he said, "This is going to be a big one. I don't know how we are going to get out of it."

At about mid-morning, we heard the rumbling of approaching tanks. I had experienced this once before, during the night, when tanks with flame-throwers had attacked us. It was a frightening and horrifying experience to see men being burned to cinders in the trenches. This time it was daylight. Soon there were tanks as far as the eye could see. Apart from the unnerving sound of the motors everything was totally quiet.

Then someone fired the first antitank gun and all hell broke loose. Machine guns could be heard everywhere. To my surprise the Canadians were not shooting from inside their tanks but had their machine guns mounted on top of the tanks. They stood up in the open lid and fired at everything that moved.

What I witnessed is something I shall never forget. Very few of the tanks were destroyed, even when they were directly hit by an antitank gun, because the guns had to be fired from very close range to be effective. Most of the time they were fired from the shoulder and many of them missed. When the Canadians saw a man in a hole, after he had unsuccessfully fired his gun, they ran their tanks directly over the hole, turned the tank about on its own axis and practically churned the man to death underneath.

Within a very short time I saw dozens of young soldiers killed by machine gun fire. By midday our lines were overrun. Those who survived were either wounded or taken prisoner. Walter and I managed to escape by jumping into a nearby stream. One of the tanks spotted us and shot in our direction. But we were submerged in the stream up to our shoulders, hanging on to willow branches, and they lost us and did not pursue us any further.

That whole afternoon we hid in the willows. We could hear and see the Canadians moving into Eibergen. Walter and I decided to stay in hiding and try to get away during the night. We were cold and wet. As it was getting dark we approached the nearest farmhouse, hoping the people would be friendly. With my heart beating fast, I knocked on the front door. The door opened slowly and a very surprised man met us. I guess that he had expected to see Canadians.

For a few seconds no one spoke. Then Walter asked the man, "Sprechen Sie Deutsch?" Instead of answering he looked nervously around. Evidently he wanted to be sure that no one saw him talking to us. Then to our surprise he asked us in German to come into the house. He appeared to be alone.

We told the man that we would like him to provide shelter for us for the night and that we intended to leave in the middle of the night. He asked whether we knew that the Canadians had occupied the village. Walter assured him that we were aware of it and that we would be grateful for his help. After hesitating for a few moments he said he would shelter us and then gave each of us a tin of homemade sausage and a small loaf of bread for food on the way. He said that he was going to let us hide in the loft above the barn and that he would leave the small barn door, facing the back, open for us to get away whenever we wished. We were immensely relieved.

Then a young boy came into the house, talking excitedly, possibly a neighbor. When he saw us he stopped abruptly. I felt a little uneasy as we made our way through the barn and up the ladder into the loft. Before we settled down to sleep we discussed our getaway plan in detail. It was decided that we would leave around midnight, make our way north along the coast, and then back into Germany. Since we were exhausted we fell asleep almost immediately.

The next thing I knew there was a knock on the door of the loft. We were both startled when we heard a voice saying, "Machen Sie auf, kommen Sie raus, Sie werden gut behandelt." (Open up and come out, you will be treated well.) In an instant, we were both wide awake, realizing it was daylight and we had missed our chance of getting away during the night. Walter whispered to me, "I don't think it was the farmer who gave us away. It must have been the boy." I nodded in agreement.

I opened the small door of the loft and saw a civilian man wearing an armband and carrying a German machine gun without the bolt. Walter reached angrily for his pistol but I persuaded him not to do anything foolish. As we were trained, I took out the bolt of my pistol and threw it away into the hay. Walter did the same with his rifle. Then we descended the ladder to the barn floor. We saw five Canadian soldiers, calling to us to come out with our hands up.

4

On April 1st 1945, I was taken prisoner. The only thing I had dreaded all through the war had come about. All the time I was engaged in combat I was never afraid of being killed, but I had an awful feeling about being captured.

My captors were big men. The one who searched me was a sergeant. He made me put my hands over my head and began going through my pockets. When he found my military pass I knew I was in deep trouble.

This is because, after we were finished with the paratrooper course, we all had to glue a picture of Hitler in the back of our pass. I cringed when I saw him look at it. First his face turned red, then he ripped out the picture and slapped my face several times. I wanted to tell him that I did not put the picture in there because I wanted to but because I was ordered to. However I could not speak any English so it was no use trying.

My friend Walter was searched not far from me. He did not have a picture of Hitler in his military pass and therefore fared much better than I did. After my pass was returned to me my captor took everything that I possessed, first my watch, then my compass, my knife and my maps. I was not wearing any rings. He did not question me because he did not speak German. However he did ask me if I spoke English, which I could figure out. I just shrugged my shoulders. To my surprise, he did not take the sausage, which the farmer had given me, nor the field bag in which I carried it.

After the initial search, Walter and I were escorted to the village, where the guard motioned us to sit down against a wall. By then it was about mid-afternoon. The whole of Eibergen was swarming with Canadian soldiers. They were sitting on their tanks drinking coffee and going about as if they were resting from a maneuver in peacetime. There were no other German prisoners in sight. We later found out that they had been captured by the hundreds and moved out the day before.

We were on the outskirts of the village. One Canadian soldier was close by guarding us. After some time I tried to talk to Walter but the guard made it clear that we were not to talk to each other. We must have sat there for about an hour when about 30 people, all civilians, approached us. They were of all ages and were carrying stones of various sizes. To our horror we realized that they intended to stone us against the wall. My heart pounded and I wanted to call out to the guard to stop them. Fortunately for us, when they came within throwing distance, the Canadian guard shot above their heads with his machine gun. They turned around and left. I have never felt more relieved in my life and sent a silent prayer of thanks to the Lord for his help.

Towards evening a tank approached and stopped right in front of us. A soldier got out and ordered us to jump on the back. A second tank followed us. We must have been going about twenty minutes when we stopped at a check station. We were taken inside a building where we were questioned and searched again. This time they were British personnel, who spoke German, and we were thoroughly interrogated. The captain, who asked me all sorts of questions about the unit I belonged to, spoke in a very soft voice. When I gave him my name, rank, and serial number, he told me that my unit did not exist any more and that those who were not killed had all been captured.

It was getting dark when we continued our trip again on the back of the tank and by the time we stopped it was completely dark. We were ordered to get off. In the distance I could barely make out the shape of a large gate. Someone called to us to run towards the gate. I could hardly see where I was going because the night was pitch black. All I heard was "Come on, come on, come on," repeatedly.

We kept running in the dark until we stumbled and fell. Lying on the ground I heard the big gate shut behind us and then I realized that we had fallen over fellow prisoners of war, lying on the ground. Walter and I huddled side by side for the rest of the night. As daylight came, we saw thousands more doing the same thing to keep warm. Looking around I saw nothing but fellow prisoners of war.

We were in this particular camp for about a week. There was no roof over our heads. We were herded together like cattle in a huge fenced-in area. British soldiers guarded the camp. To lie down at night was out of the question because the ground was too cold. The only food we were given was biscuits and water.

One morning some of the men were loaded onto goods trains. I was relieved to be one of them, because wherever we were being taken could not be worse than this. When the train finally stopped we were marched to a camp in the town of Jabbece.

On arrival we were immediately deloused. The process of delousing went like this. We were ordered to line up in single file. Then about twenty of the British guards approached us. Each was equipped with a pump, similar to a large bicycle pump. The pumps were filled with a yellow powder which they sprayed everywhere where there was an opening in our clothes; down the front, inside our shirts, down the back, up our sleeves, up through our trouser legs and finally into our fly, which we had to open. I found it hilarious but at least we were not infested with fleas.

Afterwards we were housed in reasonably good barracks. They were large, accommodating about one hundred fifty of us, a far cry from wandering around a huge field, day and night, with no cover and nothing to lie on. The barracks were packed far beyond normal capacity, but it felt good to have a roof over our heads and to be sheltered from those cold April winds.

On the fourth day in the camp we were all interrogated in detail. At this point in the war, when we all knew that it was almost over, it did not make sense any more to state name, rank and serial number. A British sergeant interrogated me. He spoke fluent German and spent about ten minutes with me, asking me anything from what I thought about Hitler to details of the unit I had served in. He also wanted to know all about my education, the time before I became a paratrooper, and where I did my basic training.

At the end of the questioning I couldn't believe my ears when he asked me if I would like to join the British air force. I was promised immediate freedom and the same treatment as any other British airman. I later found out that many of us who had been in the air force were made the same offer, including my friend Walter. Both of us declined, although some did accept the offer because they had no family and no home to go to after the war. If my friend Walter had accepted I would not have held it against him because he came from the eastern part of Germany where most of the people had been driven from their homes by the Russians.

Some days after the interrogations all of us who were flying personnel were separated from the rest and put into a concrete building at the edge of the camp. We were held behind locked doors. Rumors were spreading that we were going to be handed over to the Russians. Walter was very fearful. He confided in me, "If these rumors turn out to be true, I will escape before we are handed over to the Russians, no matter what happens to me."

When the doors were unlocked after three days we were again marched to the train station at Jabbece and loaded onto a goods train. The morale amongst us was very low. No one wanted to end up in Siberia.

The carriages we were transported in had no roofs. Every time we passed underneath a bridge, rocks and stones rained down on us from civilians standing on the bridge. Many of us got injured, though I personally was spared from being hit. One of the guards in our carriage was hit with a good size stone on the side of his head. He was furious and shot a few rounds of bullets at the people. Each time the train slowly wound its way through a small village, the same thing happened.

We were all greatly relieved when we finally reached Noordwijk a Zee, (Noordwijk on the Sea). The station was very close to the ocean. We were immediately taken to the beach and loaded on to a boat, which was nothing but a steel hull, with no amenities whatever. I knew from previous experience that I easily get seasick, so I made my way amidships. When it finally started moving we met with our escorts, who were British personnel. Although it left a lot of questions unanswered, I felt relieved to find out that we were being taken to England.

The sound of the ship's engine vibrated through the whole boat. It was difficult to find any rest. I was tired and huddled against a steel post, trying to close my eyes.

After about an hour I made my way to the bathroom. For that convenience they had about ten open 55-gallon drums lined up at the back of the ship. Everything else I leave to your imagination.

Before I got there, several of the British guards appeared, each carrying an armful of life-vests. They laid them down and motioned to us to put them on. I happened to be in the right place at the right time because I was handed one of the life-vests, although there were not enough for everybody.

We were then informed through an interpreter that there were German submarines in the area. Shortly after that we heard a deafening noise and felt a terrific vibration going through the ship. Everyone jumped to their feet and shouted, "Torpedoed!" There was a big panic among those who had no life-vests.

Then a guard appeared with an interpreter and told us to calm down. He explained that the captain had dropped anchor and also that we were being escorted by the British navy to ensure a safe passage.

All night long we lay at anchor out in the Channel. In the early hours of the next morning we continued our voyage. The sea was getting very rough and a lot of us became seasick. Since there were no windows the ship smelled terrible. I was feeling sick myself and hoped we would soon arrive at our destination.

In the evening we finally arrived at the port of Dover. The landing flap at the back of the ship was lowered onto the beach and we were quickly unloaded. It felt good to breathe the fresh sea air. Before we got to dry land we had to wade knee deep through the water. We were assembled on the beach by about 25 guards and escorted to a train station, where there was a passenger train waiting for us.

The guards divided us into groups of 100 and then we filled carriage after carriage until we were all on board. There were about four guards in our carriage, two at either end. About an hour and a half later our train arrived at a station in London.

We were unloaded and taken to a large hall, where we had to take off all our clothes, including underwear. The only things we were allowed to keep on were our shoes. All of our names and ranks had to be registered, then we continued in shoes and 'Adam's costume' in single file through the hall. Then we had to remove our shoes. The guards looked inside and we were allowed to put them back on.

A little further on we met with a group of guards who stood behind a large pile of underwear, socks, jackets, and trousers. No one asked about size and no one bothered to see if what we were given would fit. All they did was reach down, pick up an item, and throw it at us.

Consequently, most of us ended up with clothes that were either too small or too large. I myself had a pair of trousers that were far too big around the waist and way too long. Since we had to leave our uniforms behind we had no belts to hold our trousers up.

Our clothes were British army uniforms, dyed chocolate brown. At the back of the jackets an area of about 14 inches in diameter was cut out and replaced with a bright yellow patch. Similarly, a piece of material about 10 inches long had been cut out of the knee area of each trouser leg and replaced with a bright yellow patch. This way everybody could identify a German prisoner of war from a long way off.

Many of us exchanged trousers or jackets. I found someone to swap trousers with me. Now they fit around the waist so I didn't have to hold them up.

We were reassembled and, flanked by our guards, were taken to the next train. Before we boarded, we were given some food and water to drink. The train was again heavily guarded.

As we rolled out of the station I felt a little more secure for the first time since my capture. At least I was in British hands and was being taken to a more permanent camp. Judging by the sun we were traveling north.

About mid-afternoon the train stopped and we were maneuvered onto different rails off the main track. There we all got off, formed a long line, and were given some hot soup by a British army canteen. As we got back into our carriages it was getting dark and we realized that we were going to spend the night there. We learned from our men who could speak English and made conversation with the guards that we were going to the county of Yorkshire in the north of England.

It would take one more day of traveling. I think that was the most comfortable night I had spent so far; we were dry and it was reasonably warm.

Early the next morning we were maneuvered back to the main line and before long we were on the last leg of our train ride. After another full day of traveling we finally reached our destination.

The guards reassembled us in rows of three, side by side in military formation. I noticed the name of Otley in the train station. Heavily guarded, we set off marching through the village. Little did I realize then that my life was about to take a dramatic turn and that in a small village close by was a young girl of 16, who would one day become my wife.

As we were marching through the village we all started singing German songs. The streets were lined with curious onlookers. Word must have got out that more German prisoners were to occupy the prison camp at Otley. After marching for about three-quarters of an hour we saw a large camp ahead. There seemed to be hundreds of tents covering the slopes of a hill. A high fence with rows of barbed wire surrounded the camp and I noticed several guard towers which were occupied.

.

Otley, England

5

When we arrived at the camp the big gates were opened, we were assembled inside, and they were closed behind us again. We got our first look at our new camp commander. He informed us through an interpreter about the rules and regulations of camp life. Then he made our mouths water by telling us that we would be receiving three hot meals a day. What that really meant, we soon found out.

We were divided up in groups of 100 men. There were ten tents in a row with ten of us occupying one tent, which was built to accommodate three British soldiers comfortably. So when ten of us lay down to sleep, our legs crossed in the middle. It was especially uncomfortable for those with long legs. I happen to have short legs, so if I pulled them up just a little, no one crossed mine.

Our beds consisted of a thin sack filled with straw lying directly on the bare ground. The British army had wooden platforms so that the air could circulate underneath their straw sacks. It was not long before our sacks started to rot underneath us because the ground was very damp.

Everything apart from the sleeping area was in the open, washrooms and toilets, etc. We had no belongings except for that which we wore. One knife per tent was issued each morning to divide the food.

For breakfast we had a cup of porridge with a little black tea. The porridge came in a galvanized container large enough to feed 100 men. However, 80% of it was water. Besides this we only got one slice of bread to last us all day, along with some more tea. In the late afternoon we received a little butter and a little cheese and again more tea. The butter and cheese was about one inch square and had to be divided among ten of us. So much for our three hot meals a day.

There were working commandos for those of us who did not have a rank. According to the Geneva Convention, no one with a rank could be made to work unless they volunteered. This meant that I didn't have to go to work if I decided not to.

We could either work for a farmer or in a brickyard, where they manufactured clay bricks of all kinds, and dozens of varieties of pipes. These were then fired in very large ovens, in temperatures of up to 120 degrees Fahrenheit. The ovens had to be loaded and unloaded at maximum temperature because they couldn't afford to cool the ovens down and then heat them up again. I was fortunate not to have to work in a commando like that because those who were assigned to such jobs burned their eyebrows off in the intense heat.

Gradually my fellow prisoners were assigned to working commandos. The majority of them worked for small farmers. They were all right because they received food from the people they worked for. The rest of us were getting very weak. So it didn't take long until I also volunteered to go to work. We were promised a bigger daily ration if we worked.

One morning I was asked to help out preparing food for the kitchen. There were about 20 of us sitting at tables, which were arranged in squares, with two guards watching us. We had to take the leaves off cabbages to prepare them for cooking. The guards had to make sure we didn't eat anything.

I kept my eyes on both of them and when I thought they weren't looking in my direction I quickly stuffed a small cabbage leaf under my shirt. So before we were through I had tucked away quite a few leaves. That would be something to fill my empty stomach. I hoped that we would not be searched before we returned to our tents. Luckily all went well. Back in my tent, I had to find a place to eat my cabbage leaves without being seen by anyone. Otherwise I might be reported by one of my fellow prisoners. Such things happened.

Our camp held about 3000 men. Next to us, separated by a 10-foot high fence, was another camp with a capacity of 2000 men, and then a much smaller camp, which held only navy and army officers. I learned that a lot of these officers were submarine commanders who had obeyed the British order to bring their submarines into a designated British harbor and surrender.

There was a forbidden zone of ten feet on either side of the fence, which we were not allowed to enter and we were not permitted to talk with anyone on the other side of the fence. Once it happened that a man from our camp saw his brother in one of the adjacent camps. Their joy was so great that they both ran to the fence and one of them was then shot dead by a guard. The next morning during roll call, we were told that the guard had overreacted and had been relieved of his post.

Life in the camp became very boring. Many hours in the day we just walked around to get a little exercise and to pass the time.

April 16th was my birthday. I was 21 years old. Throughout the day I was very quiet and withdrawn. My thoughts went back to my home, my family, and my brother who was a fighter pilot, flying an ME109. Although we never heard any news, everyone knew that the war could not go on much longer. I wondered how far the allied forces had penetrated into Germany and how my family was faring. I had not heard anything from them for a long time. My father and three sisters were at home and I hoped they were all right. My mother had died of pneumonia during the war.

The weather became very wet. It rained without stopping for about three days. As the camp was situated on the side of a hill the water started rushing down through our tents. Those of us who were not yet working sat huddled in our tents shivering, but at least we managed to keep dry.

Those who were out working, however, and being transported back and forth on open trucks, were not so fortunate. They were soaking wet when they arrived back at the camp. There was no place to dry anything, so they had no choice but to lie down at night wearing their wet clothes, hoping they would be dried out by morning. We had only one set of clothes, so there was nothing to change into.

As the rain persisted, we were given a spade and pickax, one set for each ten tents. We were expected to dig a trench around each tent so that we could dry out. The problem was that we were so weak none of us could dig for more than five minutes at a time. The trenches proved very helpful as it rained on and off for the rest of the month. Many of us got sick with colds and other related problems. In the early days of May we finally dried out.

One morning at roll call I was assigned to a farm commando with another three men. We were given a tag with the number 78 on it. That was our commando number by which the farmer would recognize us.

The next morning all the working commandos assembled near the gate. They were then picked up in horse-drawn carts, small pickup trucks or even cars.

Our farmer arrived in a Morris Minor station wagon. We held up our card showing the number 78. The guard checked the farmer's card and then opened the gate to let us out.

Without saying anything, the farmer motioned to us to follow him. He was of medium build and rather small for a farmer, with a weather-beaten face and rugged appearance, but he had kind blue eyes under his bushy eyebrows. He wore long rubber boots covered in mud. The four of us greeted our farmer with, "Good morning"— we knew how to say that—and then climbed one by one into the station wagon. After we had driven about 20 minutes, no one saying a word, we arrived at a medium size farm.

The farmer pulled up in the yard outside some horse stables. After we got out he turned to us and asked the inevitable question, "Do you speak English?" We shrugged our shoulders and said, "No." I did understand some English by now so I said, "A little." From that moment on I was selected as spokesman for our group.

The farmer had many horses. The manure in the stables was so high that he could hardly get the horses through the doors. It looked as though they had not been cleaned out for years. It was our job to remove the manure and carry it in wheelbarrows to an enclosure away from the house. We were very weak but we tried to do the work as fast as possible because we wanted to make a good impression.

By about midday we were pretty exhausted. It was very hard work forking up manure because it must have been packed down over a period of several years.

From the time we started working the farmer was busy somewhere else. When we saw him again he told us to take a break. We sat down to rest and for quite some time he stood there watching us. Then he asked where our lunch was. We shrugged our shoulders and made him understand that we had none. He then told me that he wanted to see our jackets. After checking all our pockets and finding nothing, he went back to the house and came back with a letter from the British Command. He showed me where it said that we were being well fed in the camp and need not be given food. I tried to explain to him that we were given only one slice of bread a day. With an astonished look on his face he went back to the house.

Since we didn't know how long a lunch break he wanted us to take we decided to start working again after we had rested for about 15 minutes. Just then the farmer arrived. He was carrying a huge plate full of sausages. They were freshly fried and smelled delicious. Not far behind him came his wife with two bowls full of French fries. Both the farmer and his wife stood watching us in amazement while we were consuming this delicious meal, and we couldn't say, "Thank you," enough. The meal was then followed by a nice cup of hot tea. How good it felt to have a full stomach after going hungry for so long.

The rest of the day we worked harder than ever. I was hoping that this job would last as long as I was a prisoner of war. Unfortunately it lasted only two weeks. When we returned to camp one night we were told that we wouldn't be returning to the farmer. The officers from the adjacent camp had decided that they wanted to go to work. There were other commandos, but they preferred the small jobs with the farmers. We had to give way to the officers' request.

6

One morning I was informed that I had been assigned to a new commando. At 7:00 a.m. prompt, 30 of us climbed onto the truck, which had pulled up outside the camp. We sat in three rows on wooden planks facing the front of the truck. I soon realized that it was going to be a very windy ride. The truck was open and there was nothing to protect us from the cold wind. We must have driven about half an hour when we arrived at a village called Clayton.

We stopped in front of an old abandoned farmhouse. There were tractors, cement mixers, as well as gravel, cement, and piles of curbstones and wooden planks around the building. We were shown into a room in the old farmhouse where we could leave our jackets if we wanted. The room had some crude benches and tables. In the corner was a tea urn, that is, a round copper container with a tap at the bottom. It was used to make hot water for tea.

A man entered the room with an interpreter. The interpreter introduced him as the engineer in charge of the building site and told us that our place of work was to be a housing estate. The houses to be built were called council houses. We, however, were to build the roads and manholes and lay the water and sewage pipes.

Before we started work they wanted to know who was a bricklayer, who could drive a tractor or a dump truck, and who had ever laid pipes before. To my surprise quite a few men put their hands up.

I myself was made a trench digger. There were two huge caterpillar tractors, which had already dug the outlines of the roads, and one machine, which dug the trenches, but a lot of hand digging was still to be done. We were introduced to several civilians who worked for the contractor and were to be supervising us. My foreman was called Jack. He wore a shirt without a collar. Around his neck was tied a red handkerchief and his trousers were tied with a string above his boots. I figured he was in his early fifties. He was very small and chewed tobacco.

We shoveled and dug all day, wrestling with sticky wet mud. The weather was fair but cool. About 5:30 p.m. the truck arrived to take us back to camp. On our way home it started to thunder. There was no place to shelter as the rain pounded mercilessly into our faces.

By the time we arrived back at the camp the rain had stopped. Since I was soaked through I walked around the camp, hoping to dry out a little before I lay down on my straw bed. The evening breeze helped somewhat, but my clothes were still very damp when I settled down for the night.

This sort of thing happened quite often. After a few days at the building site, digging, driving tractors, and working in mud, I longed to be working on a farm, removing manure from horse stables.

The building site we worked on was flanked by nice homes. Occasionally, when we happened to be working close by, some nice lady would come out and hand us a cup of tea. But only when she thought that she was not observed by anyone, because we were strictly forbidden to fraternize.

One morning, after we arrived at the site, the engineer told us through an interpreter that he needed more bricklayers and more men to lay pipes. Besides that he was looking for three carpenters who could build supports for the deeper trenches and do general timberwork, such as framing manholes.

I used to build model airplanes and even helped to build full-size gliders in my teens, so I was handy with wood. Since I was not too thrilled about working in dirt and mud, I raised my hand and said I was a timber-man. I nudged my friend Walter who stood next to me and motioned to him to put his hand up too. He said, "Ich hab doch keine Ahnung von Holzarbeit," (I have no idea how to work with wood). I figured I could show him the things he didn't know and finally he volunteered. One more timber-man put his hand up. After that, everyone was told to go about his assigned tasks.

The three newly assigned timber-men, however, were taken into the office to be introduced to the man who would be our supervisor. He was an elderly person who, I supposed, had worked as a carpenter all his life and was now hired to finish his working days on the building site. He introduced himself as Bill and outlined what the job entailed. My English was sufficiently improved by now to understand simple conversations.

Bill showed us a blueprint of all the manhole positions. There were quite a lot of them. We were also shown a detailed blueprint of a manhole frame. Since I was a tool and die maker by trade I had no difficulty reading and understanding technical drawings. It was decided that I was to build the manholes with the help of my friend Walter. The other timber-man would reinforce the trenches to prevent them from collapsing before the pipes were laid.

I was given a saw, a claw hammer, a ruler, a setsquare, and a packet of nails. We went to work building our first manhole. Bill was with us most of the time and showed us how to go about it in a professional way. However, he liked to take a lot of tea breaks in his office. He was a friendly person and we got on well with each other. We learned that he had lost his wife and was living alone.

There was a narrow road running through the building site, which connected the two main streets on either side. It was frequently used by the people who lived in the nearby houses. I was working a lot near the walkway and I especially noticed a teenage girl who came by once or twice a week, always around the same time, which was about 4:30 p.m. to 5:00 p.m., just before we got ready to go back to camp. I only ever saw her from a distance, but I wanted to get a closer look. I guessed she was about seventeen or eighteen years old.

One day, as she was coming in my direction, I made it my business to be near the road, pretending to do some measuring. As she walked by I managed to get a good look at her. She was very pretty, just a little smaller than I, with beautiful blue eyes, which seemed to sparkle. Her hair was dark blond and fell neatly to her shoulders. She had a beautiful complexion and was very dainty in stature. She must have noticed that I was looking at her because she blushed slightly. As she walked on, my eyes followed her all the way.

Driving back to camp that evening, I couldn't get the picture of that cute little face out of my mind. We had strict orders not to fraternize and were told that we would be severely punished if we were caught doing so. So my common sense told me to leave well alone.

A few days later, however, I saw her again, this time holding a small girl by the hand. I decided that I was going to talk to them, so I made my way over to the walkway. I would pretend to be busy measuring; it seemed the most sensible thing to do. I had to be sure that no one saw me but when they were just about level with me I looked up at them and said, "Good evening."

The girls gave me a quick look and also greeted me with a "Good evening." Then they seemed to quicken their pace a little. As I walked back to the manhole I kept glancing in their direction and noticed that at the very top of the building site they went into a house together. The small girl I assumed to be a relative.

That night I could not go to sleep for a long time. I had the urge to learn English properly. How I was going to go about this, I didn't know. Perhaps Bill, the foreman, could help me if I conversed with him as much as possible.

The next day I found many reasons to talk to him. I also told him that I wanted to learn English and asked if he would help me. He seemed very pleased with the idea. So, whenever I wanted to know a word, he would tell me how to pronounce it. But I wanted to write it down too.

One day, when I was talking to Bill about words, I asked him if he had something to write on. He handed me a pencil and a piece of scrap paper from his office. I started writing and he made sure I spelled the words properly. Before long I had many pieces of scrap paper with words on them. I looked after them as if they were gold.

7

One evening we heard a lot of gunshots and fireworks in the nearby village of Clayton. One of the guards who was walking outside the fence called out to us, "The war is over! The war is over!"

Next morning, May 7th, we all had to assemble. The commander himself told us that Germany had capitulated and the war with England was over. We were all relieved and now the question on everyone's mind was, how soon will we be sent home?

I wondered if my family was OK and if our village had been badly damaged. Not knowing was almost unbearable. One thing was certain; there would be no celebrating or fireworks in Germany.

Next morning on our way to work we had a lot of stones thrown at us, mostly by kids. The British population seemed different. Naturally, they had won the war. After we had arrived at the building site it was decided that it had been a mistake to bring us out and we were taken back to the camp.

On our way back, as we were going up a steep country lane, a young boy about 12 years old threw a stone at us. The driver stopped the lorry. Two of our men jumped off, threw the boy onto the back, gave him a good spanking, and then dropped him off again. The driver smiled, made the victory sign, and drove on. Except for an occasional incident while waiting at stop signs, the ride back to the camp went smoothly.

During the day we spent a lot of time sitting in our tents, thinking and talking about what it would be like to be sent back home. Little did we know that most of us would spend another three years behind barbed wire. All day and into the early hours of the next morning we could hear fireworks and celebrating in the village of Otley.

The face of that young girl kept coming into my mind. I wondered what her name was, where she lived, and how old she might be. Since she crossed the building site so often I assumed she must be living close by. If only I could find a way to communicate with her. My heart told me I had to do something. Why, I don't know. I knew nothing about the girl. And why would she want to have anything to do with a German prisoner of war?

My growling stomach told me that I had to find ways to get more food for myself. One Sunday we were all given a piece of raisin cake. It tasted delicious and I saw an opportunity for some extra food. I made a bet with one of the men in our tent called Bruno that I would jump off the water tower, which was situated in the corner of the camp, if he gave me his piece of cake. During my school years I had always been a little daredevil.

Accompanied by a few more who had listened in on our conversation we walked over to the tower. After I climbed up to the top and looked down I realized it was probably a very foolish thing to do. But I had had good parachute training and was fairly confident that I wouldn't get hurt. During my fall I was concentrating on what I had to do when I hit the ground. When I landed I thought my legs had ended up in my chest. For a few moments I couldn't move. But I was all right, and very reluctantly I was handed my piece of cake.

Since I was getting weaker physically and always felt hungry I devised another way to get a good source of food besides the watery porridge, which we got every morning for the so-called breakfast.

Just for something to do, I walked a lot around the camp. One morning, on one of my walks, I noticed that the empty canisters, in which our porridge had been made, were put outside behind the kitchen. The tubs into which the porridge was poured contained 80% water. However the original containers still had a residue of good porridge left in them. So I made sure that no one was looking and then I jumped the fence enclosing the kitchen. What a feast I had, wiping my hand around the inside of the container and licking the good porridge from my hand.

For a long time I managed to do this almost every day, early in the morning, without being detected. It helped me to keep up my strength.

One day, we were informed that changes were to be made which would benefit us. We now had a shop where we could purchase items such as pencils, toothpaste, toothbrushes, and paper. There was also a Cassell's German-English/English-German dictionary. We received seven pieces of plastic money a week to spend. This would buy a pencil in a week, a toothbrush in two weeks, and so on. I figured it would take me six weeks to buy the dictionary and I made up my mind to save up for it. The dictionary was more important than the toothpaste or toothbrush, and I already had scrap paper and a pencil from Bill. Then I had another idea. If I sold my piece of cake on Sunday, it would speed up the process.

One Friday morning at the building site, Bill called me into his office. He told me that the night before, after we had gone home, they had dug a trench across the public walkway. He wanted me to build a wooden bridge over it because the walkway had to be kept open for public use for the time being. Bill had drawn a sketch on a piece of paper and he gave me instructions on what to do. He had already delivered the wood that I needed with a dump truck and he left me to it. The bridge had to be just wide enough for one person to cross safely.

In the afternoon it started to drizzle. At around 4:00 p.m. the bridge was ready to be used, except for the railing. As I looked down the walkway, I noticed someone with a raised umbrella coming towards me. It was the young girl I had named 'Pretty' because I didn't know her name.

Quickly I made up my mind that this time I was going to get a good look at her. As she got close, I turned my back to her, pretending that I didn't know she was there. She had to say something because there was no other way for her to get round. For a few seconds she stood behind me. I did nothing. Then she said in a quiet voice, "Excuse me, may I come by?"

I thought what a sweet voice she had. I stood up and my eyes met hers for a brief moment. She had a beautiful face. I could not miss her deep blue eyes. Standing next to me I noticed that she was about half a head smaller than myself, she had a good figure and I could even smell her perfume. Her hair was dark and she had high cheekbones. I felt a great urge to touch her cheeks. Now that I was so close she looked more beautiful than I had imagined.

I motioned to her to go across. I even managed to say, "Please." I was tempted to offer my hand and help her across, but I didn't dare. As she walked on, I saw her glance back at me and smile. My heart beat faster and I felt as if I was walking on air for the rest of the afternoon.

That evening, after I lay down to sleep, I couldn't get that lovely face and those beautiful eyes out of my mind.

The more I thought about the young lady I called 'Pretty', the more I realized how much I liked her. I wished that I could talk to her. But then I wouldn't know what to say, not being able to speak the language.

I kept myself busy writing words on anything I could find to write on, including toilet paper. We were issued about two feet of it every day. I also acquired a candle and some matches from Bill. He brought them to me when I told him that I needed them for writing after dark. Nearly all of the men I shared the tent with, except Walter, worked in brickyards. They were a lot more tired than I was, and the candlelight didn't stop them from going to sleep. I was glad because I used to sit up till very late at night, teaching myself English and writing it all down.

One weekend I sold my piece of cake, which gave me enough plastic money to buy a red pen and a scrap book. Now I could write my German words in black and the English equivalent in red ink. After a while I had quite a collection of words.

The manhole frames were coming along very well, but there were many still to be built. Bill seemed very pleased with the progress. As the so-called 'chief timber-man' on the building site I was more or less free to be anywhere on the site I wanted, without being questioned. The guards, as well as the civilian staff, got to know me well. But still I had to be very careful what I did. I was afraid that if anyone suspected that I intended to fraternize I might be transferred to another work commando and never see my 'pretty lady' again. My mind was continually working on ways to communicate with her. So far, besides saying, "Excuse me" and "Please" we had only had eye contact.

8

One night, as I lay wondering what I could do, I got the idea of exchanging notes with the young lady. I would carefully drop a note in front of her in the hope that 'Pretty' would pick it up as she was walking by.

As I was going towards the office that evening I noticed a cigarette box lying on the ground. I bent down to pick it up. To my surprise, it was half full of cigarettes. What a find. To get them inside the camp, I decided to put them loose under my shirt and throw the box away. On second thoughts, I tore off the back of the box and took it with me, to write on.

That evening I sat up in my tent with the candle burning. I wrote *Have a very good night, Charlie.* I assumed that Karl must translate as Charlie.

For the next few days I carried the note around with me, waiting for the right opportunity. Finally, one Friday afternoon I saw 'Pretty' coming up the walkway. There was not much activity near the little bridge I had built, so I decided to drop the note near there. I wanted to look as if I was doing something so I carried a piece of wood in one hand and the note in the other. When I thought the moment was right I dropped the note about five feet in front of her as I crossed over the road. I kept on walking but I knew that she had seen the note. At first she walked past it, then stopped, took one step back, looked around and then bent down to pick it up. My heart leaped with joy as I watched her walk away with the note.

The next Monday afternoon I saw 'Pretty' coming across the

building site with the same little girl who was with her once before. I started to walk in their direction and saw the little girl drop a small package on the ground. I continued walking until they were some distance away from me, then, after making sure that everything was clear, I turned and walked back to the spot. Pretending I had something in my shoe I knelt down, took off one of my shoes and at the same time retrieved the packet.

I couldn't wait to find a suitable place behind a wall where I could be alone and open it. Besides a sandwich, I found a note which read, *Thank you for your note, enjoy the sandwich. Sue.* I was very hungry, so I sat down and enjoyed the food. Now I knew that the girl's name was Sue. Only much later did I learn that it was short for Ursula.

9

The following night I didn't sleep much. I was going over and over in my mind what had happened during the day. I still couldn't believe that it was not a dream. If only I could write a note to say thank you for that delicious sandwich.

For the next few days I carried a note for Sue around with me, hidden in my shoe because that was the safest place. One afternoon, as I was busy building a frame for another manhole, I saw someone crawling towards me on hands and knees along one of the dry stone walls that covered the building site. [Eventually they would all have to come down to make way for the houses.]

Sue was standing some distance away. The little girl kept looking in all directions, wondering if anyone would see her. She came up to me and handed me a paper sack, saying, "From my cousin." I remembered the letter in my shoe and quickly took it off and handed her my note. As I was doing so, I asked what her name was. She replied, "My name is Kathy." Then she turned around and crawled back along the wall. When she got to the road she got up and ran towards Sue who was waiting for her. I could hardly believe what had happened.

Kathy was a cute little girl, about seven years old and very bright. At least some of my concerns about communicating with Sue had been settled. I started to wonder if Sue really liked me or if she was only taking pity on a German prisoner of war.

I couldn't wait to see what was in the sack. To my surprise, it was a whole small loaf of bread and a packet of cigarettes. As I was always hungry, I ate most of the bread. The rest I managed to hide under my jacket. The army jackets were short and very loose with a tight band at the bottom, very handy for hiding anything small without it falling out. The cigarettes fit neatly in my jacket pocket.

I went back to the trench where Walter was working to share the bread with him. Of course he was curious to know where I had obtained it. I answered, "Never mind, a little bird gave it to me." He looked at me a bit strangely but he did not press me any further and enjoyed the bread.

Similar exchanges took place every few days. We handed notes back and forth between little Kathy and myself. As my English improved our notes became short letters. I was very much afraid that she might be seen or get caught. I had to be constantly alert.

Finally I had enough plastic money to buy a dictionary. Every evening after that, when I returned home from the building site, I would sit in my tent and study new words and phrases by candle light, mostly the words which I needed to write my notes. Everything I wrote was of a general nature, such as 'Thank you for the cigarettes and goodies,' or, 'I hope your cousin Kathy is very careful.'

One day Sue wrote that her mother knew she was seeing me and writing to me, but her father didn't. It seemed that her mother approved of what her daughter was doing. That made me happy.

Sometimes we would see each other in Bradford while I was on my way back to camp and she happened to be in town, riding her bicycle as we drove by. Then she would mention it in her next note. She was naturally inquisitive about the conditions at the camp. So she would ask 'Are you warm at night? Do you have a nice bed to sleep in?' Sometimes it took me two or three evenings to compose a small letter because I had to look up most of the words in my dictionary. Also I wrote the way we think in German and no doubt it was not always easy for her to figure out what I was trying to tell her.

One Monday we were just getting ready to call it a day at the building site. The truck was waiting at the usual place and most of the men were already seated on the planks. I saw Sue hurrying towards me and I sensed that she had something for me. However I was still quite a distance away and all the men were waiting for me to get on the truck. My mind was feverishly trying to come up with a feasible

29.TH OKT. 45

MY DEAREST SUE
×××××××××

J HAVE JUST MET KATHIE
AND GOT YOUR VERY SWEET AND LOVELY
LETTER. TAKE MY BEST THANKS FOR IT.
J AM VERY PLEASED TO HEAR ANY NEWS
ABAUT YOU AFTER A LONG WHILE OF
WAITING. WE CAN'T ANY WORK TO-DAY.
THEREFORE J CAN ANSWER YOU AT ONCE.
ON THURSDAY J GAVE A LETTER FOR YOU
TO KATHIE. DIDN'T SHE HAND IT OVER TO YOU,
OR DID YOU FORGET TO MENTION ITS RECEIPT
IN YOUR LAST LETTER? "CHAMPION" J SAY
TO YOUR TOFFES AND MANY THANKS FOR THE
CIGARETTES.

DEAR SUE YOU WERE ILL?
ALL THE TIME MY THOUGHTS WERE WITH YOU.
J WOULD ASK KATHIE ABOUT YOU. BUT THERE
WERE SOME OBSTAKLES TO DO SO. NOW THEN.
J AM GLAD TO HEAR THAT YOU ARE FIT
AGAIN. J AM VERY SORRY MY SWEETHEART
NOT TO HAVE SEEN YOU ON THE BUS.

MY DARLING J AM VERY
DELIGHTED THAT YOU ARE SO MUCH ENDEAVOU=
RED TO FULFILL MY DESIRES. BUT NOW,
WHAT MAY J DO ANY GOOD FOR YOU?
JT'S A PITTY THAT YOU CAN'T ADDER ONCE
AT NOON OR IN THE AFTERNOON TO PAY
ME A VISIT.

MY DEAR NOW IT IS 8 O CLOCK.
JUST J AM COMING BAK FROM BRADFORD
AND WILL WRITE TO FINISH THIS LETTER.
J WAS VERY SORRY THAT YOU HAD TO GO HOME
SO FAST LAST NIGHT. MY LORRY ARRIVED AT
½ PAST 7 A.M. WOULD YOU HAVE GONE BAK
IF YOU HAD KNOW THIS??

PLEAS TURN OVER

My first letter to Sue

FOR TO DAY I WILL HAVE TO CLOSED NOW.

LOTS AND LOTS OF LOVE
AND THOUSAND OF KISSES
YOUR FRIEND

I LOVE YOU.
Darling

excuse to delay the truck. Sue was still 20 yards away from me.

Then I remembered the shoe trick. I quickly took off one of my boots and my sock while the truck driver blew his horn impatiently. I called out that I had a splinter in my foot and wouldn't be long. Finally Sue caught up with me, sitting there on the ground, and a letter fell right in front of me. Without looking up I slipped it inside my sock and put my sock and boot back on again. I did not look back at Sue, but hurried to jump onto the back of the truck.

One of the men nearest to the cab gave the usual signal that we were all aboard, and off we went. I later found out that Walter had kept the driver talking, to distract him from what was going on. Walter was aware of the relationship between Sue and me, and he was ready to help out whenever the need arose.

By now we were on friendly terms with the driver and he was very good to us. Many a time, when we were driving through town, he would slow down to show us something of interest. Once, when one of our men had problems with very sore eyes, probably from the wind and draught from riding on the open truck, he stopped at a drug store and bought him some eye lotion.

After we arrived back at the camp that evening we were all told to wait inside the gate. We were searched occasionally after returning from work but I was not sure if this was routine or if they had got word that someone was trying to smuggle something in. The guards checked all our pockets but I was not asked to take off my shoes and the letter went undetected.

Some time later I looked for a place where I could read my letter. Sue had a lot more to say than usual. I read that her cousin Kathy had got into trouble at her school for going near prisoners of war at the building site. She was told that her parents would be notified. All the children were warned not to go anywhere near us.

Naturally neither Sue nor I wanted Kathy to get into any more trouble. Sue suggested that we should not exchange any more letters for a while, to let things cool off. I thought that was a good idea, and in the meantime I would try to think up a better and safer way to write to each other.

I suppose the way we had been exchanging letters was a little too obvious. Sooner or later someone was bound to find out. I was very glad that no one was pointing the finger at me. Perhaps someone was shielding me? My foreman Bill seemed to like me very much and if he suspected anything he never said so. Also, there were more than 50% of the manholes still to be built.

10

The following week or so I spent a lot of time studying English and writing it all down. I also helped with a project to beautify our camp. Each tent was involved in making the surrounding area looking neat. It was almost like a competition. There were two large piles of white and pink gravel stones in one corner of the camp. They came in very useful for creating all sorts of pretty shapes and fancy entryways. In fact, the whole camp looked much better than it had when we first occupied it. I think the camp commander liked the way we kept everything so clean.

I was still taking my early morning walk before breakfast and stopping to clean out the empty porridge containers. In the meantime I had managed to carve a wooden spoon to make it easier for me to scrape out the canisters. For a long time the porridge residue in those canisters was the biggest meal I had each day.

One day I realized that my mouth was infected. It was covered with a yellow film and I had difficulty eating. So one evening, after returning home from work, I reported sick. I was told to be at the main gate the next morning at 8:00 a.m. There were several of us who needed to see a doctor. A guard escorted us to the nearby hospital. This consisted of a small Nissen hut in which the consultations took place, and two large tents, full of what looked like rollaway beds.

After the doctor had looked at my mouth he admitted me for treatment. So for the first time since I was captured I got to sleep in a bed. I was given some pills to take; I suppose they were antibiotics. What I liked best about being in hospital was that three times a day I got a hot drink. It tasted very good and I was told that it was similar to a spread called Bovril, which can also be used as a sandwich spread or to flavor soups. We also got more food than in the camp and every morning we got a good bowl of porridge for breakfast. I thought, it almost pays to be sick in a prison camp. But even so I would rather go back to my job as a timber-man and see my young lady occasionally.

On my first evening in hospital the other patients told me that an officer from the adjacent camp was going to come and read to us as a form of entertainment. They said he was quite interesting.

The next morning an officer walked in and greeted us with a cheery "Good morning." I had the biggest shock when I realized that he was none other than the lieutenant who had deserted our company. I wondered if he would recognize me. While he was entertaining us he kept looking in my direction.

When he was finished I stretched out my hand to shake his and said, "My name is Kern, Karl Kern." I felt like saying, "Remember, you sent me to the battalion headquarters when you deserted your company and left me to lead them out of the mess." But I knew it wouldn't make any sense to bring it up. He said he thought he had recognized me and we talked for a while, but he never mentioned anything about the past. After that he left and I never saw him again.

Three days later my mouth had cleared up and I was escorted back to the camp.

Back at the building site Bill wanted to know if I was OK. Walter had told him that I was in hospital. But he hadn't seen Sue at all.

The whistle blew to announce the lunch break. As I walked towards the old farmhouse I met Bill who said he was going home early and would I take care of things until he was back the next day? I assured him everything would be OK.

While I was having my cup of tea I suddenly thought of an answer to our correspondence problem. I was so excited about it that I didn't wait for the whistle. I murmured to the others that I had to catch up on some work and left.

To make myself look busy, I headed towards the top of the building site with a hammer and a piece of wood. There, near an old empty pigsty and close to the walkway, was the only place where the landscape made a dip. Otherwise the building site was level.

I walked beside the dry stone wall, which ran about 90 degrees from the walkway, looking for a stone in the wall, about five inches high and ten inches wide, which could easily be removed. The idea was to pull out the stone, put a letter behind it, and put it back in place. No one would know any different and we would have a 'mail box' which was not visible to the rest of the world. It would be our own private 'post office.' We could arrange a certain day, say, twice a week, when we would put a letter inside.

After looking up and down the wall for a while I found just the stone that I needed. It was about half way up the five-foot wall and could be removed without any difficulty. All I had to do now was mark the stone on the surface, so that Sue could find it. I used my claw hammer to make some gauges which would be visible enough, but not too obvious.

Now I had to make a small, easy-to-understand sketch for Sue so that she could find the stone. I measured the distance from the stone to the walkway as ten paces. In my letter I would say twelve paces because she was smaller than I and had shorter legs.

For the rest of the day I was very excited about our new mailbox. This had to work out. It was our only chance.

11

All through the evening and late into the night I sat in my tent by candlelight with my dictionary, putting together a letter. Sue had to be able to fully understand it. I also had to tell her that I had been in hospital for three days, in case she was looking for me and wondered where I was. There were still quite a number of walls crisscrossing the building site, but I hoped she would find the one opposite the empty pigsty. It was the only small structure left on the whole site. Also there was a good chance that it would be left standing for a while yet. Most of the building activity was still some distance away. So it was not buzzing with workmen and building traffic. It had to be ideal for our "mailbox."

All next day I was nervous. More than once I walked over to our newly created mailbox, looking at it from all different angles, trying to figure out how it could be seen from the nearby houses. I came to the conclusion that it was the only suitable place on the whole building site.

I carried my letter around with me all day. When the coast was clear I walked by the wall, pulled out the stone, and put the letter inside. It worked perfectly and there was plenty of room behind it. I wished I could just leave it there, but this one I had to hand over personally.

During the afternoon I went into the office to find out from Bill, in a roundabout way, when the rest of the walls on the building site would be pulled down. He told me that they were concentrating on completing the bottom area of the site first. All water mains, manholes,

Sunday, 2'nd-de
1945

My Dearest Lue,-
x xxx x x x x x x x / x

After a long
waiting I will write some lins
to You. I did believe to get answer
from You, but I didn't get one.
Haven't You got the letter I sent
by Betty. You can't believe
my Dareing how I was waiting
for some lines of You. All the
time we couldn't see one another
I was with You with all my
thoughts. I can't forget You - and
my heart would breake if I
couldn't see You. I want I should
be with You always and You
would stay at me for all time.
My Sweetheart, we
are at Butsherhill since one week.
Here it is better than in Otley.
We have woodlouses with electric

II

light and overs.

My Darling Sue, I am very pleased that I was seeing You some time in Bradford and on Saturday, but sorry I couldn't talk to You. I think You had a letter for me.

My Dear Sue, all the time I have thought about the problem how we could send us our letters. I will give You a good advise where we can put our letters and fetch them. I think it would be the best to put our letters into the wall, beside the path which leads over the fields. It is the same path which You passed on Saturdays You did visit me. That You can better know what wall I mean, I must

III

say You that it is distant some feet from the small corrigated iren-house. The place is at the inside of the wall in the corner. We put then the letters behind a stone, that is marked with a white colour. Then we will look every day to this place. How do You think it about this advise? Or do You think it would be to dangerous? I will try to send this letter at anyway to You my Darling. So I beg You to send me an answer that I can see if You like my advise. For to-day I will have to closed now.

Lots and Lots of love
and thausand of Kisses
Your best friend

P. T. O.

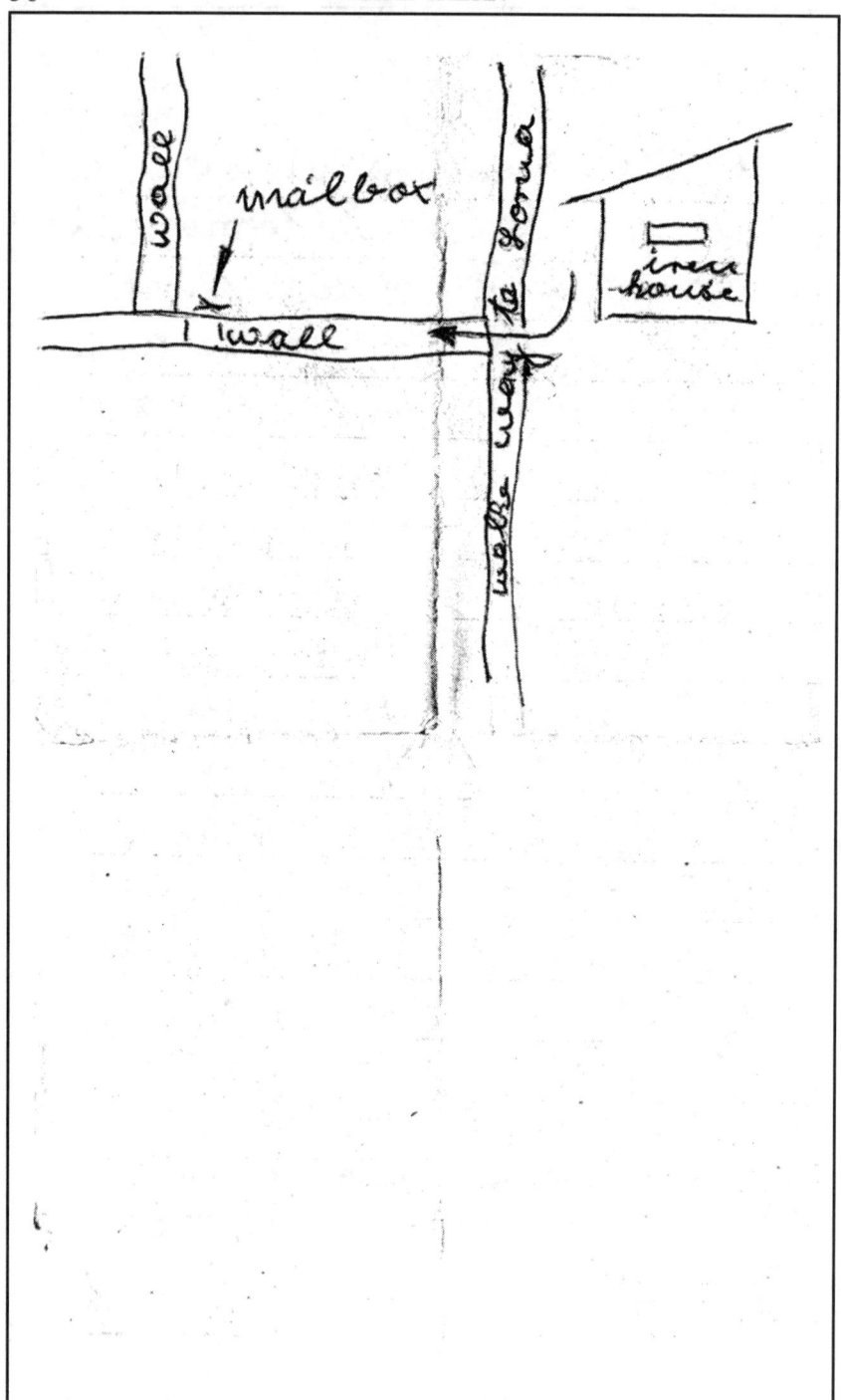

pipes, and curbstones had to be in place before the year-end, so that they could start building the council houses. Then they would start working on the top end. That was good news. Hopefully, we should be able to use our mailbox for the rest of the year.

Late afternoon I finally saw Sue slowly coming down the walkway. All we had to do now was to make sure that we were not seen exchanging letters. I was more nervous than usual because of what had happened to her cousin Kathy.

As she came closer the whistle blew, indicating that our workday was over. This was good because everyone was busy leaving their work places, making their way down towards the office, and concentrating on going home. I walked down the path towards Sue and dropped my letter beside her. She bent down immediately to pick it up and at the same time she also dropped a letter. I stopped to let her walk a good distance away, before bending down to pick it up. Then I sat down to put the letter inside my sock.

I was more than relieved when I took my place on the back of the truck. After arriving back at the camp we all had to assemble. My first fear was that we were going to be searched. As it turned out, we were given a preprinted card. It was explained to us that this card would be mailed to our next-of-kin notifying them that we were in British hands. All we had to do was to write in a mailing address. We were allowed to cross out words, which didn't apply and leave what applied.

In my case it read as follows, *I am a member of the defeated German army. I am in British hands. I am alive. I am not wounded.* We were allowed to sign our name. Our relatives could then return the other half, which was also preprinted. The address of our camp was already printed on it. This way they were able to notify us about conditions at home.

In the meantime my family had received an official notification from the German government that I had been killed in action. The card, which was addressed to my father, read as follows, '*This office has the sad duty to inform you that, according to a report which we received, a member of your family by the name of Karl Kern, who was born April 16th 1924 in Eningen, was killed in action between the 21st and the 28th of February 1945. Place of death was Weeze, Rhineland. The location of the grave is the military cemetery at Weeze, grave No. 26. The office at Eningen, which registers all deaths, was informed of this today, the 25th of January 1946. For a copy of the death certificate please contact this office. Any further information regarding this is not available.'* The card was dated April 21st 1945. I was not aware of it until two years later.

Over the weekend I spent a great deal of time studying English. Most of us were also busy filling out the card. It had to be handed in by Monday morning. Many of the men had no home address because their families had to leave everything behind, fleeing from the advancing Russian army. They had no idea where any of their family members were.

After the great trek from the east, mainly with horse and cart containing their few belongings, the refugees were put into camps by the thousands in the northeastern part of Germany. They were classified as displaced persons. I was thankful that my family didn't have to leave. We lived in the south of Germany near the city of Stuttgart.

The first sign of life from me to my family

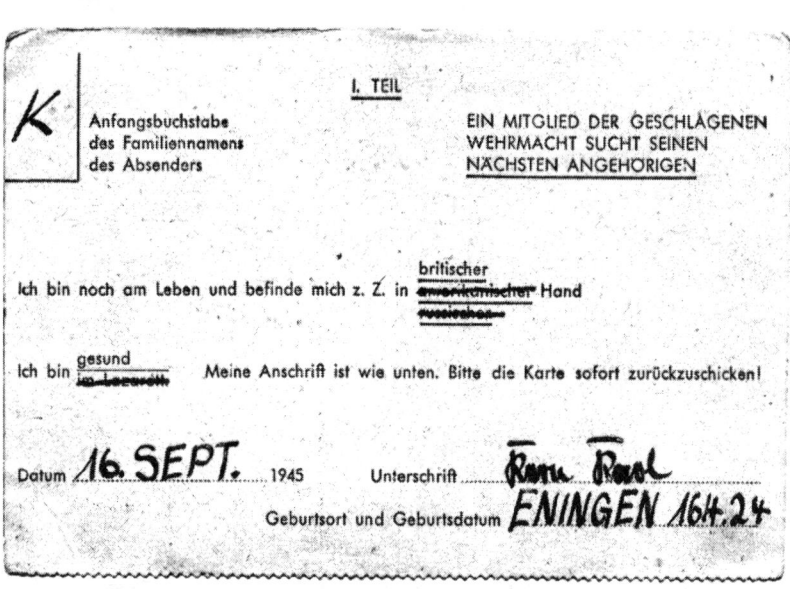

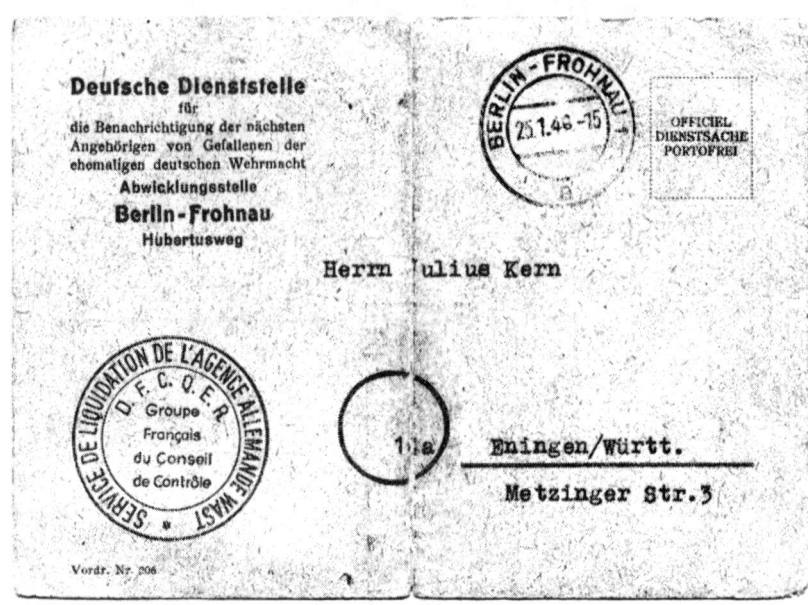

The notice to my father that I was killed in action

12

Monday turned out to be one of those rainy days. We got a good soaking going to work. Then it drizzled all morning. I was glad that I didn't have to work in the dirt and mud, although I had to help Walter and the other timber-men to reinforce the freshly dug trenches, so that they wouldn't cave in before the pipes were laid.

By around noon it was raining so heavily that all work had to be halted, and everyone was allowed to take shelter in the old farmhouse. I took the opportunity to spend time with my foreman Bill in his office. He had his potbelly stove burning, so it felt very cozy. He always had a kettle standing on the stove for hot water, so we shared a nice cup of tea while we were talking about the work to be done.

During our conversation Bill mentioned the incident at school. He said that the girls were warned to stay away from here. I had the feeling that he knew more than he was willing to admit.

I managed to change the subject by asking him about some words in English and their proper meaning. I told him that I now had an English dictionary, which helped me a great deal with my learning. He was very pleased about that. I also mentioned that we were allowed to send word to our families to let them know we were OK. This brought him around to telling me that the guards had been instructed to keep a close watch on anyone fraternizing. I could see that he was concerned for me.

After about two hours the whistle blew, which meant the rain had stopped and everyone was to return to his respective work areas.

Several of the manholes, that I had built the wooden casings for, had been completed by the bricklayers. They were partly brick and partly cement, with steel bars built into the side, to act as a ladder. Bill took me over to see one and I climbed down into it to see what it was like. I was quite proud of myself to actually see the results of my work. After that Bill went back to his office.

Before returning to camp I had to check to see if Sue had understood my letter and found our secret letterbox. In case someone was watching I pretended that I had to do some measuring. Then I slowly made my way over to the mailbox and removed the stone. To my surprise and delight there was not only a letter but also a pack of cigarettes behind it. In spite of the heavy rain everything was dry.

I walked a few steps away, sat down, and pretending I had something in my shoe, I put the letter inside my sock. The cigarettes I put into the pocket of my jacket.

The trip back to the camp was dry. Our clothes were not too wet, just damp. We were always glad about that, because there was nothing more miserable then having to lie down at night in wet clothes.

I had to find a place to read my letter before it got too dark. I lit a cigarette and went for a walk because I didn't want to read in the tent. I would have to wait too long for that.

Sue told me what a wonderful idea it was to create a mailbox. She was relieved to know that we didn't have to use her little cousin any more to exchange our letters. I was pleased with myself that I had managed to write a letter she could fully understand. Among other things, she mentioned that she and her cousin, Lorna, had gone together to the building site to look for the mailbox. Her cousin thought I must be a genius to come up with an idea like that. In reality I was just an inventive prisoner of war who had fallen in love with a cute little English girl.

I was sure that I was in love. I had heard of people falling in love at first sight, but they usually had a chance to talk and get to know each other. We had never had as much as five minutes together, nor had I ever held her hand. Yet my heart started beating faster every time I had a chance to see her. It must be love.

However, I couldn't help but wonder how I would ever be able to convey my thoughts and feelings to her. My vocabulary was so very limited. I didn't like to think of the possibility that she might not have the same feelings for me. Also I had no idea where I would end up when the work on the site was completed. I had to try not to let these thoughts bother me too much for the moment.

Sue had mentioned in one of her letters that on a Tuesday she was with her aunt in a village called Pudsey. Her Aunt Phyllis told her that every evening she noticed a truck full of German prisoners passing right by her house. So she asked me to look out for her next time. She would be standing at the side of the road.

This gave me something to look forward to for the next day. Since I didn't know on which side of the street she was going to stand I would make sure that I was sitting at the very back of the truck. This way I could see both sides of the street.

The following Tuesday evening, on our way back to the camp, I kept a good look out, so that I wouldn't miss the village. After about 20 minutes I saw the name Pudsey coming up. It looked like a very nice place. All the houses were detached. As we entered the village I saw Sue standing at the side of the road. As we drove by her I raised my hand just a little and waved. She waved back and all of a sudden a lot of the men sitting towards the back of the truck were waving to her. Of course they didn't know that we knew each other. This moment was my treat for the day. If nothing else, at least I had seen her.

On Friday evenings, rush hour traffic moved slowly through Bradford. It was also the time when Sue often had errands to run there. She knew which streets we drove through, so she always stood where she could see us going by. We dared not wave at each other. She told me that some boys once saw her waving as we drove by, and they threw stones at her. So we only exchanged looks.

All the manholes were almost completed. The roads were also finished and the contractor had started to build the first homes on the site. The days were getting colder and the nights were miserable in our tents. My straw sack, which was my bed, was almost falling apart. I began to feel the bare ground underneath me. I was not looking forward to the winter.

Our mailbox was working flawlessly. We managed to send two letters almost every week and Sue kept me supplied with cigarettes and sandwiches. Our letters had now become love letters. We yearned to be in each other's arms. Sue finished a lot of her letters with 'BOLTOP,' which meant *better on lips than on paper*.

13

One morning Bill called me into his office. He told me that very soon most of our commandos would no longer be needed, mine included. The second phase of the building project was going to be started, but would not be ready for pipes and manholes until the spring of 1946.

Two days later, a bulldozer flattened the wall, which contained our mailbox. My heart sank.

Back at the camp, I received the news that my last day at the building site was to be the following Tuesday. I had to let Sue know. Before going to sleep I wrote a short letter, telling her that I was being moved to another place of work. I had to take the letter with me to work on the Monday, hoping that I would see her and have a chance to give it to her. To my dismay I also learned that I would be moved to another camp.

On Monday I made my way up to the area where our mailbox had been. I wondered if there was a letter from Sue behind the stone when they pulled the wall down. But everything had already been cleared away.

At 4:30 p.m. the whistle blew, and there was still no sign of my sweetheart.

With a terrible sadness in my heart I climbed on the truck and we drove back to the camp.

All that night I barely closed my eyes. Over and over I wondered how I could let Sue know that I would not be able to see her any more. As I lay on my bunk, feeling sorry for myself, I suddenly remembered that the next day was a Tuesday, which meant that Sue would be at her aunt's house. A spark of hope came back into my aching heart. This was my chance to get my letter to her. Perhaps I could throw it from the lorry right in front of her. But that would be too risky. I had to find a better way.

By Tuesday I was ready to take more of a risk than usual. Before the whistle blew for the last time I had a plan. Since this was our last day at the building site most of us were busy cleaning tools and machinery. I took my friend Walter to one side and told him what I had in mind. I needed him to help me carry it out. I also contemplated including the driver. He had been very helpful and friendly in the past. But I abandoned that idea because if he did not go along with it my plan would be foiled completely.

As we approached Pudsey my heart beat faster. My friend Walter was sitting right behind the cab of the truck. I was sitting at the very back.

Sue was standing at her usual place by the side of the road. At the right moment I sneezed very hard so that my cap, which was sitting loosely on my head, fell off into the road right in front of Sue. At the same time Walter started hammering on the top of the cab. The driver then rolled down his window and asked what the hammering was for. Walter shouted to him to stop the truck because one of the men had lost his cap.

The driver stopped. Meanwhile, Sue had run towards the cap lying in the street and picked it up. I jumped off the lorry and ran towards her. At the same time, I saw a young man from the nearby gas station also running toward Sue. Luckily I got there before him. [Sue told me later that he was cross with her for picking it up]. While Sue handed me the cap I passed her my letter underneath it and said, "There is a letter, be careful." Then I ran back to the truck and climbed aboard. Walter told the driver that everything was OK and we pulled away. I had accomplished another almost impossible mission and my heart was pounding all the way back to camp.

14

About three days later some of us were loaded on to trucks and transported to another camp near Leeds, about twenty miles away. The address was: Leeds 6, Butcher Hill, near West Park.

With winter approaching, I was not sorry to get away from the rotting straw sacks and the uncomfortable small tents. This camp was a lot smaller, holding about six hundred men. The nice thing about it was that we were housed in wooden barracks, which had potbelly stoves for heating. There were about fifty of us in one barrack and we had bunk beds and straw sacks to sleep on. The stoves were located in the middle of each barrack so if we got wet going back and forth to work, at least we had a place where we could dry out our clothes. I felt like a king with this kind of comfort.

The guardhouse was next to the camp entrance. We had a staff sergeant in charge of the camp and four young guards. The camp was situated next to a large farmhouse. There were no towers manned by guards as we had had at the Otley camp. Along one side of the camp there was an unused railway line. Between the camp and the rails were heavy barbed wire fences, except in one place where two freight cars stood. Each freight car had a small window, about one square foot in size. The wheels had been taken off and they were used to store bales of straw.

Next to the farmhouse was a deep quarry, and on the edge of it was the camp kitchen. There was no barbed wire on that side of the camp because the quarry was almost straight down and very deep. The barrack in which I lived was in a corner of the camp, close to the railway lines. These lines were not level with the camp, but about ten feet or so below it.

Considering the fact that we were prisoners of war, the place had a good atmosphere, and I felt more like a human being again. I think I would have really enjoyed the camp, if it hadn't been for the fact that I was 20 miles away from Sue and I had no idea when I would see her again. I had to let her know where I was, and for that I needed to find out the exact geographic location for myself.

After two days in the camp I walked around it, trying to figure out where we were, and how I could relate this to Sue. I came to the conclusion that it was impossible unless I went outside the camp. The only thing that separated us from the outside was the barbed wire, the gate at the entrance and the guards occupying the guardhouse. To do anything during daylight was out of the question, it had to be at night. I made up my mind which part of the barbed wire I would go through and which direction to walk in. It was crazy but I was determined.

Around midnight I quietly got out of my bunk and made my way towards the barbed wire fence. I intended to make notes of the location such as street names, or names of any building that could easily be recognized. I had with me a pencil and a piece of paper. It was very dark and no moon or stars could be seen in the sky.

During the day I had noticed that at one point the barbed wire was fastened to a wooden post with heavy staples. Using a piece of steel that I had found earlier, I managed to remove the barbed wire from the lower section of the post, just enough to be able to crawl through. After about ten minutes of prying and pulling, I was finally outside the camp.

I walked through some meadows. There were small shrubs around, which I could barely make out in the dark. I had to move very slowly because I wanted to be as quiet as possible.

During the day I had seen people walking back and forth near here so I knew that I would come out on a road. I followed this road until I came to a built-up area. The first crossroads that I came to were dimly lit, but I could make out some street names. On my paper I started to draw a sketch of what I saw. Not too far down the road I came to a bus stop, which was just outside a hotel. This became the focal point of my sketch. With the name of a hotel, a bus stop, and the names of two streets at the crossroads, the area could be found.

I got back to the camp after about an hour and hooked the barbed wire back onto the post again, so it would not be noticed. Then, instead of heading straight home, I sneaked into the nearby toilets and then walked out of them, back toward my barracks, just in case anyone saw me and got suspicious.

I now had some good information that I hoped would help Sue to find the camp.

After a few days I was assigned to a different commando. It was a big brickyard called Higgs and Hill. Quite a few of our men already worked there. The yard was packed with a hundred different shapes, styles, and sizes of clay pipes. I was assigned to load delivery trucks together with the supervisor. I also had to check the pipes for any faults or cracks.

The brickyard was about half an hour's drive from the camp. Not far from the brickyard was a sugar refinery, where some other of the men worked. We all rode together in the same truck.

At least once a week the boys who worked at the sugar factory managed to smuggle a small bag of sugar out. Since there was no chance of anyone getting a bag of sugar past the guards, the boys had an agreement with the driver that he would slow down before they got to the camp entrance. Then they simply threw the bag over the fence, to collect it after dark. In order to hide the sugar from the guards, we had loosened some of the floorboards in the barracks to put the sugar underneath. The driver also got his share of the sugar, for his part in slowing the truck down.

After working at the brickyard for a few weeks, I approached the foreman to see if he would mind mailing a letter for me. I told him that I had some friends in Clayton who had known my family for a long time. He said he would.

The letter was already written, so I put it in an envelope, addressed it, and gave it to him the next morning. I was aware that if the foreman opened my letter I could get into serious trouble. On the other hand, if I tried to sneak out of the camp during the night to find a mailbox, it could be just as dangerous. Whatever I did was risky. Somehow I felt that I could trust the foreman. The next day I asked him if he had mailed the letter for me and he said, "Yes."

Christmas of 1945 went by without any fanfare. I wondered how everybody in my family was faring. It was several months since we had been allowed to send a card through the British government to let our families know that we were alive. None of us had heard anything from home.

Many of us were busy making all sorts of toys from wood and toothbrushes. I managed to find a piece of Plexiglas, which I shaped into hearts, and I also started to make a bracelet for Sue. Some of the men, who worked at the sugar refinery, brought home sacks, which they stripped, thread by thread, and shaped them into very nice slippers. Since we now had a stove, we could burn small holes into toys for linkages, or we could burn patterns into carved ornaments.

Once a month a civilian was allowed to come into the camp. He would buy our toys and pay us. We had a small shop in the camp, which was open every Saturday. There we could purchase a newspaper, books, writing paper, and toothpaste.

The last few weeks had been very painful for me. I missed seeing Sue so very much. Day after day I looked out for her, especially at the weekends. I had told Sue in my letters to follow the rails to the camp, and I had suggested that she should try to come on a Saturday or Sunday. I was hoping there was a bus that she could take. The same rule applied here as at the old camp, we were not allowed to go closer than ten feet to the barbed wire. So if Sue made it to the camp, I would need someone to watch out for guards.

So far, there had been no other opportunity for us to write to each other. We were simply not allowed to receive any mail. Anything addressed to us would be confiscated.

Many a night I dreamed that I was outside the camp in Sue's arms. The days and the weeks went by and nothing happened. My heart was heavy because I had not seen her, nor heard from her for such a long time.

Ever since the first few days at the camp I had made friends with two of my fellow prisoners. We quickly grew to like and trust each other. Every weekend and some evenings, we sat or walked together, talking about our past and sharing prison camp life. Their names were Seppie and Heinz.

Seppie came from the southern part of Germany. He was a few

years older than I and had served as a corporal in the German army. With his black hair and exceptional good looks, I imagine he would at one time have turned any girl's head. He sang in operas and I was always hoping that some time I would be able to hear him sing. He was quiet and polite and very likeable. I could never imagine him being a fighting soldier.

Heinz was younger than I and a little smaller. His hair was blond and with his keen blue eyes one could guess that he came from the northeastern part of Germany. He was a lot more boisterous than Seppie. Anything exciting appealed to him and in many ways he reminded me of myself in my younger days. Heinz had also served in the German army, though he was too young to have any rank.

I decided it was time to let them both in on my secret love affair. By now I knew them well enough to trust them. So one evening, as we were walking around near the perimeter of the camp, I said to them, "What I am about to tell you must be kept very secret."

"Mach es nicht so spannend, lass mal hören, was so wichtig ist, dass man es geheim halten muss," blurted out Heinz, (Don't make it so dramatic and let us hear what it is that has to be kept so secret).

I told them the whole story about Sue, how I met her and that we used to write to each other at the Clayton building site. They were astonished. Then Seppie said, "How can we help?" I pointed to the barbed wire and told him that was the place where I went out one night to find out where we were and then sent a letter to my young lady, with a sketch showing the location.

Seppie said, "Do you really think she is going to come here from that far away?"

"The way I know her, yes," I replied.

They both asked a lot of questions but then promised to keep it all a secret and that they would help me in whatever way I needed them.

"This is going to be very exciting," remarked Heinz before we split up and said good night.

My Darling Sweetheart Sue,
x x x x x x x x x x x x x x x

I thank you very much for your lovely letter, which I received on Tuesday night from Lorna, and I hope that you also have got my letter. I am very sorry my Darling, that I couldn't see you on Tuesday night on the bus, before you are going to pudsey. I have look out for you but I think, that you was not yet there. We have passed the bus but already at quarter past 5 o'clock.

My Darling when I have read in your letter that you will go to pudsey I tryed to send my full address of our camp so that it was possibly your to visit me at the camp. But sorry I had not opportunity to give this letter to Lorna.

My Sweetheart, I am very pleased to hear that you will try

II

to visit me at the camp and I
hope, that it will be possibly you,
to do that soon.

My Darling Sue, I am very
sorry, that I must tell you not to
come on a Sunday, but on a Saturday to night. You must understand,
that it isn't possibly me to meet
you ton another time! The best way
would be for you, to come with a
girl of me to camred which comes
every Saturday to our camp to
visit him. The address of this girl
is: Shirley Coulson
                208, Clayton road
          lidget green
                   Bradford.
It is the doughter of the police-in-
spector from Bradford. He don't
know ofcourse, that she comes to
my camred.

My Darling if you
dont like to come with this girl
I will write you the full address

III.

of the camp. Our camp is leeds 6
Butcher-Hill near westpark.
It is just near a stone-mind.
If you come alone from leeds go
past our camp down the Hill.
I am waiting for you about 200
yards after our camp on a tree.

But the best way would be for
you my Dear, if you are coming
with the girl, because our camp
is very bad to find.

My Darling I hope now,
that you will understand me and
that you will have time to visit me
on the Saturday this week.
The time I mean the hour when
I am waiting for you is 7:30 p.m.
If it isn't possibly you to come,
try please that you can write it
me befor Saturday.

For to-day I will have
to close now in Hopes, that
we can see us on Saturday-night.

III !

With ~~lots~~ ~~lots~~ ~~lots~~ lots of love
and thousand of kisses
~~ten~~ ~~ever~~ Your always loving
                                        friend
                                                 Karl

~~their keep it~~

P.s. ~~remember it love~~
      Tell Lorna the name of
my conrad is Heinz. I shall
send from him many greetings
to her.

I am waiting
for you
Darling

I love you
Darling
so very much

please turn over

My Darling, excited with
please, that I have written you
not more. I have had not
much time.

So good night
ontill Saturday

Darling —
so very much

15

One Sunday the men were playing soccer as usual. And as usual I was walking near the corner of the camp, looking down over the fields in the hope of seeing Sue.

I could hardly believe my eyes when I saw someone coming towards the camp along the railway lines. I could tell it was Sue from the way she walked and moved, as I had watched her so many times at the Clayton building site. She was still quite a distance away.

I quickly ran to find Seppie, who I knew was waiting in the barracks in case I needed him. I whispered to him that I needed his help at the fence. He came right away. Then I walked over to tell Heinz whom I spotted watching the soccer game. The stage was set. Both of them would keep a look out for the guards or any one who was likely to report me.

As I got closer to the barbed wire and saw Sue coming up the embankment towards me, I suddenly realized that this was the very first time we would actually be able to talk with each other, even though the coils of wire on each side of the fence kept us at least 6 feet apart. Seppie and Heinz had taken up positions behind me, facing the camp. I went as close to the barbed wire as I possibly could on my side, and so did Sue on the other side.

I could tell that Sue was very nervous, and so was I. At first we just looked at each other. She looked absolutely beautiful to me. For a moment I completely forgot that I was standing inside a prison camp behind barbed wire. Then Sue said, "Hi Karl, how are you?"

With a shaky voice I answered, "Hello Sue, I am fine, I can't

believe you actually found the camp and I am so pleased to see you."
I warned her to be careful that no one saw us and added that two
friends of mine were keeping a look out for guards.

She reached into her handbag, took out a letter, and threw it over
the fence. I picked it up and hid it under my jacket. After the letter
followed a packet of cigarettes and some sandwiches. Then she told
me that she came to the camp two weeks before, with her cousin
Lorna. However, it took them a long time to find it, so when they saw
the camp in the distance they went back home, as it was getting late.
Sue had so much to tell me and she was talking so fast that I had to
ask her to speak more slowly.

I could hardly believe that we had actually talked for over five
minutes. Sue told me that her mother knew she had come to visit me
and had seen my letters, but her father did not know about me. She
kept looking around nervously for fear someone would see her. She
then said, "I came by bus and got off at the bus stop in front of the
hotel which you mentioned in your letter. It took me almost two hours
to get here". Finally she said, "Oh Karl, I am going to have to go back
home, I will come again."

I thanked her for the cigarettes and sandwiches and asked her to
give my greetings to her mother. She then blew me a kiss through the
fence and turned to leave. As she went down the embankment I called
out to her, "I love you, please come back soon".

She turned around to say, "I love you too Darling."

As I watched her going back along the railway lines I felt I was in
seventh heaven. Now I knew that she loved me. She turned to wave
once more, and then she was gone.

My two friends joined me and we looked for a quiet corner to
share the sandwiches. I thanked them for their support. They were
almost as excited as I was that everything had gone according to plan.
Heinz remarked, "Man, is she ever pretty."

"You were supposed to look out for guards, not look what Sue
was like," I replied. I was certainly very glad I had them as friends.

I could hardly wait to read my letter. So while Seppie and Heinz
went to watch the soccer game, I made my way to the barracks. The
men were busy making toys and did not take much notice of me. I lay
down on my top bunk and read my letter several times over. When I

didn't understand a word, which happened quite often, I reached for
my dictionary and tried to figure out the correct meaning.

I was in love with a girl I knew practically nothing about, except
that her name was Sue Ridgway, she lived on Pasture Lane, Clayton,
and she was in nursing. I had no idea about her age or her birthday.
Come to think of it, she knew even less about me. And yet she had
come 20 miles to a POW camp, at the risk of being caught. So she
must be in love too.

The thought scared me a little, because of the difficulties that
were still ahead of us.

My English was gradually improving. Whenever I had the chance,
I would study and teach myself. Once a week one of the men in our
barracks would read and translate the newspaper to us. That way, we
got to know what was happening beyond the barbed wire. I envied
the man who could read and translate at the same time. I made up my
mind to learn the language well enough that I could express to Sue
the way I really felt.

In the evening of that eventful Sunday I answered Sue's letter.
Now I could tell her how much I really loved her, and how I longed to
be close to her, as far as my limited vocabulary allowed.

It was almost a year now since I had been taken prisoner, and
also a year since the war ended. I wondered when we would be
repatriated. I was almost hoping it wouldn't be too soon. If I was
back home in Germany we could write to each other without
restrictions, but how would we be able to see each other?

The following day I asked our yard supervisor, John, if he would
buy some postage stamps for me. I told him that I had the money to
pay for them from making and selling toys at our camp. He promised
to bring them the next day. A postage stamp at that time cost tuppence
ha'penny [two and a half pence].

The next day John brought me the stamps I asked for. He was a
man of few words. Except for things to do with the job he never
asked me any questions. However, I sensed that he was not prejudiced
towards us Germans. I asked him one day if he had any family. He
replied that he had a wife and a son who was in the army and stationed
in Germany. His son did not have bad things to say about my country.
I told him that I had a father and three sisters and he asked if he could

mail something for me, which caught me by surprise. I had planned to go outside the camp during the night to mail my letter, but this would be less risky for me. So I said I would be grateful if he mailed a letter for me and hoped for the best.

16

Two weeks went by and I wondered if Sue had received my letter. I was so deeply in love and could hardly wait to see her again.

During my walks around the camp I noticed a small opening in one of the freight cars where the straw was kept for our sleeping bags. If we were able to talk to each other through that opening there would be less chance of being seen. No one had mentioned to us that it was forbidden territory.

The freight cars had no doors facing the camp. They were both filled with straw, one was packed to capacity and the other was about three quarters full. I went inside the second one and looked through the small window. It would be ideal. There was enough room for Sue to stand on top of the embankment and I was hidden from the guardhouse. However, I could easily be seen from the area where they played soccer.

I decided to rearrange the bales of straw. I took some of them away from the corners and stacked them up in the middle so as to narrow the gap in the door opening. I left just enough room for me to get in and out easily. Then I put two bales below the small window, which I could stand on and see out comfortably. After I was done I walked over to the soccer field to make sure it was properly camouflaged.

Then I went to find Heinz and Seppie, to tell them about my plan. Seppie thought it was a brilliant idea. He mentioned that there was to be a soccer game the next day, which was a Sunday. All I needed now was for Sue to come. There was a good chance she would, because it had been two weeks since her last visit.

The soccer game was well under way when I caught sight of Sue coming along the rails. I told Heinz, who was watching the game. He immediately got into position. I waited until Sue came very close, then I motioned to her to continue following the rails. Then I headed for the freight car. Once inside, I waved through the small window and asked her to come up the embankment. So far so good.

After Sue had reached the top we were so close that we could almost touch each other. She had brought me cigarettes, a loaf of bread, and some postage stamps. I had asked her in my last letter to bring me the stamps.

How wonderful it felt to see Sue again and to be so close to her. She told me that they had started to bulldoze the roads at the top half of the Clayton building site, and that she really missed seeing me there.

I so wished I could crawl through that small window and put my arms around her. However I managed to put one of my arms out to touch her face. Sue put her arm through so that I could kiss her hand. She whispered that she loved me and missed me so much.

We must have talked about 20 minutes when I suddenly heard voices. They seemed to come from two directions. I realized that there were guards approaching from both sides of Sue. She said, "Oh Karl, they are coming for me." It was too late to get away. They called out to her to stay where she was. As I turned away, I saw Sue running down the embankment towards the rails. I think she did that because she didn't want them to see me.

I was almost sure that they were also coming for me. I managed to hide the bread, cigarettes and letter, which Sue had brought me, underneath a bale of straw. While I was doing this I heard the guards talking to Sue, but I could not hear what they were saying. I wished with all my heart it was me they caught, instead of Sue.

I was just getting out of the carriage when I saw two more guards approaching. I quickly stepped back inside. Then I peeped through the opening to watch the guards. For about five seconds they both stopped to watch the soccer game. This was my chance to get out. I took a big leap outside, made a few more quick steps, and joined the rest of the men watching the soccer game. I acted as if I had been standing there all the time and I don't think any of them realized what had happened.

Over my shoulder I could see the guards searching through the bales of straw for a prisoner. Little did they know he was standing only a few feet away from them.

After a while I was relieved to see them going back in the direction of the guardhouse. I tried to listen to what was happening to Sue, but everything was quiet. I pictured her being questioned in the guardhouse, but then I dismissed the thought because I knew they could not arrest a civilian. However it made me terribly uneasy to think I could not do anything for her.

Sadly, I started back to the barracks. I met Seppie and Heinz, who apologized for not being able to warn me in time. It was obvious that someone had reported us. This bothered me very much because it could happen again.

It was getting dark, so I told Seppie and Heinz that I had hidden some things inside one of the rail cars, and the three of us went for a walk. We had to be very careful. When they were sure that all was clear they gave me the signal to go. I climbed inside and retrieved the cigarettes, bread, and letter. We then walked on until we found a quiet spot to share the bread. We were always ready for something to eat and it did not take long until the whole loaf was gone. Then we all lit a cigarette and made our way back to the barracks.

Sue told me later in a letter that the guards wanted to know the name of the prisoner she had talked to. She told them that she didn't know. They also asked her where she lived and what her name was. She gave them the wrong name and address. Then they told her never to come near the camp again or she would get into serious trouble.

Some time later I found out what may have happened on that fateful day. I learned from a friend of mine who worked in the kitchen that the farmer who lived next to the camp had a daughter of about 17 years old. He had seen her talking through the fence with some of our men. He evidently disapproved, so occasionally he watched the camp

through binoculars. It seemed reasonable to assume that it was this
farmer who had reported us. It made me feel much better to know
that it was not one of our men.

17

My birthday was coming up and I had a daring plan for it. Part of it
was suggested to me by the friend who worked in the camp kitchen,
whose name was Theo. I mentioned to him that I would like to get
out of the camp to meet with Sue and he told me that he could probably
arrange to get me a uniform, which was worn by Polish volunteers.

These were young people, originally members of the former Polish
military, who defected to Germany after the occupation by Russia,
and then switched to join the British army. Many of them did not go
back to their homeland but stayed in England. They wore the same
uniform as the British except for the epaulette on their shoulders,
which was plain, and they did not show any rank on their sleeves.
That way, they could be identified as being Polish.

We discussed all this in the kitchen one evening while no one else
was there. I noticed that there was no barbed wire outside. Theo told
me to open the window and I saw that there was a sheer drop all the
way down into the quarry. So there was no need for barbed wire.

I told my friend of my plan to get out of the camp in broad daylight,
by going through the window. Naturally, he told me that I was crazy.
I explained to him that where I grew up in Germany there were many
rock faces and mountains. I learned to climb as a small boy and was in

my element in such a challenging environment. Coming back into the camp would be relatively easy because I intended to wait until dark and go through the opening in the barbed wire.

Now I had a lot of planning to do. I was so excited.

First I wrote a letter to Sue to let her know that I planned to meet her on Sunday, April 12th . The meeting place would be near the street that crossed the rails, about a quarter of a mile from the camp and about a quarter of a mile east of the rails. Also, I would be wearing a British uniform.

My yard supervisor mailed the letter for me the following day. [He never minded mailing my letters. I was not sure if he ever guessed that they were addressed to my sweetheart].

Then I told Heinz and Seppie, who were surprised at my plan but assured me they would do whatever they could to help. They also wanted to know who my friend in the kitchen was so that they could contact him if need be.

It was a beautiful day. The boys were playing soccer. Seppie, Heinz and myself were sitting on the ground next to the field.

Seppie was telling us of his intention to create a camp choir. He already had a few volunteers for it. I thought it was a great idea. I liked to sing myself, but for the moment I wanted to concentrate on other things.

While we were talking, my eyes were fixed on the railway lines. I longed to see Sue, although I had very little hope she would be coming back to the camp so soon after what happened only a week ago.

Heinz got up to go and then turned back and whispered to me, "There are two girls coming up towards the camp along the rails." I jumped to my feet to see for myself. It was Sue with another girl. This time I went to the corner of the camp where we had met and talked before. I looked over at Heinz and Seppie. They said, "Go ahead. We will cover for you"

In a few minutes the girls were close to the fence. First Sue threw a letter, and then a packet of cigarettes, over the fence. She introduced the other girl as her cousin Lorna. She told me she had received my mail and would try and see me on the following Sunday. I told Lorna that I was pleased to meet her and would she please give my love to her little sister Kathy. After only a few minutes, Sue apologized for having to leave so early and they turned to go. As they went back down the embankment Sue turned to wave and then they disappeared.

I was amazed at the courage of my little Sue. I didn't think she would dare to come back to the camp so soon after what happened.

That evening I read Sue's long letter, and read between the lines that she loved me as much as I loved her. There was also a birthday card for me. I thought how privileged I was to receive a birthday card in a prison camp. Probably I was the only prisoner of war in the whole of England to enjoy such good fortune.

Sue mentioned in her letter that she especially dreaded my being found out, and then moved away, and we would never see each other again. She dreamed one night that I was being moved far away to another camp and she found herself sobbing when she woke up. Her mother had warned her, "Sue dear, if you fall in love too deeply with this boy, it could be heartbreaking for you when he is repatriated back to Germany."

So far no one knew when this would take place. There were rumors circulating around the camp from time to time but I had learned not to take any notice of them.

Before the week was out I received another birthday present. The card, which I was allowed to send home through the British government, was returned to me. It contained good news. All was well at home, which was a great relief to me. Unfortunately they were not allowed to write anything else.

As more and more cards arrived from Germany I found out that many of my fellow prisoners were not as fortunate as I. Many of them were notified that they had no immediate family left. This caused a great deal of sadness.

The man who had the bunk below me became so depressed that he tried to take his own life. I found out when I followed him into an empty shed in the middle of the night. I sat down and talked to him for at least two hours until I finally managed to talk him out of it. He then came back with me to the barracks.

One evening we were all asked into a large hut. The camp commander had a big world map hanging up. He explained to us which areas of Germany were occupied by whom. I learned that my hometown was occupied by French troops. The dividing line between the French and American occupation zones was only a few miles from my hometown.

18

The first thing I did when I woke up on the following Sunday morning was to wish myself a happy birthday. I had a good feeling about this day. The following Tuesday was to be my second birthday in captivity and I would be 22 years old. There was no table decked with flowers and greeting cards. I could not even stand the birthday card up which I had received from Sue. I would have liked to keep it and treasure it as a keepsake, but it was too risky. I couldn't even keep any of Sue's letters. Sad to say, they all ended up in our potbelly stove.

I couldn't have wished for a more beautiful day. If it had been raining I would have had to abandon the whole idea. No way could I have attempted to climb down into that steep quarry in wet weather.

I breathed the fresh spring air and noticed that the hedges and trees outside the camp were in full bloom. There were the forget-me-nots, which I had brought from work and planted in front of our barracks, and cowslips and pansies, which my fellow prisoners had planted. It gave us such an uplift to be able to tend to something which was alive and which belonged to us. It helped us to forget the circumstances we were in. All the flowers and blossoms, which I saw that Sunday morning, seemed to smile at me and say, "Good luck, Karl". A small bird in a tree just outside the barbed wire sounded as if it was singing a happy birthday song especially for me.

I walked with Heinz and Seppie for a while. I told them that I would not be coming back into camp until after dark, and they assured me that they would be looking out for me when I needed to get back inside. Then they wished me good luck and left.

On my way to the kitchen I picked some of my forget-me-nots, to take to Sue.

My friend in the kitchen was expecting me. Quickly, he ushered me into the toilet to change, in case someone walked into the kitchen unexpectedly. The uniform fit me fairly well. Theo put my prisoner of war outfit into a trash can. He said he would hide it there until I came back. All the kitchen personnel wore white uniforms and he didn't want it to be seen lying around.

By 11 a.m. I had to get going. I had arranged to meet Sue around noon and I wanted to be there first. Before opening the window for me, Theo gave me a tool, which they used to sharpen knives with. It was round, about ten inches long, and it had a leather loop threaded through the end of the handle. He thought it might come in handy to help me get a hold in difficult places on the cliff side, a sort of substitute for a climber's ice pick. Thanking him, I hung it on my wrist and climbed through the window.

The descent into the quarry proved to be very difficult. It was almost straight down and there were not many places where I could get a good hold. Since I could not see very well what was below me, I had to make a lot of blind moves until I found something to hang onto. At other times I was just hanging there trying to find a foothold. Luckily there were some small trees and shrubs, which had grown over the years since the quarry closed down.

About half way down I paused on a ledge just wide enough for me to lean back and rest my body. I was exhausted and needed a few minutes to recover my strength. My climb had been very strenuous and physically I was nowhere near as fit as I was when I used to do this sort of thing in my teens. While hanging there on the side of the quarry I thought that I would not do this for anyone but for my sweetheart, Sue.

Looking down to the bottom of the quarry, I saw that I had quite a long way to go yet, and it didn't look any easier. Before long there was nothing to hold onto, not even grass, nothing but dirt. First I tried to go sideways in the hope of finding a handhold, but to no avail. What a blessing, I thought, to have the kitchen tool with me. With great effort I managed to secure it in the loose dirt just below my knees, hold onto it, and slowly and painfully make my way down over the bare spot. After doing this several times, I came to some more small shrubs and rocks, which I could hang onto.

After that the descent became much easier and the cliff less steep. Finally I had reached the bottom of the quarry.

I sat for a moment and looked up at the cliff face. I could hardly believe that I made it down without falling. However, I did not have much time to spare if I wanted to be at the spot where we had arranged to meet at noon.

The sun was high in the sky, so I knew that 12 o'clock was not far off. Looking at my uniform, I realized that I had to give myself a good clean up. Luckily it was mostly just dry dirt and dust, which came off fairly easily.

It did not take me long to get out of the quarry. I could see the tree in the distance where we had arranged to meet. As I headed towards it I could see some small farms, but not, as yet, any people. If I did meet anyone, I was prepared. After all, I told myself, I was not a German prisoner of war, but a Polish volunteer in British uniform, so my broken English should not be questioned.

Our meeting place was close to a country lane, which I named 'Karl's Lane.' It was flanked on both sides by hedges in white blossom. The fields around were covered in daffodils, cowslips and white daisies. A peaceful feeling came over me. Being away from the camp all by myself made me feel as if I was in a different world.

Several couples were taking their Sunday afternoon stroll along this beautiful lane, but no one was taking any notice of me. I stood at the foot of the big tree, my eyes anxiously searching the countryside.

After about ten minutes, which felt more like ten hours, I saw someone in the distance, walking alone, and I knew it must be Sue. I got up from where I was sitting and started walking towards her. My heart was pounding so fast that I thought it would jump out of my chest.

Before long we were in each other's arms. I held Sue tight and kissed her passionately. She whispered, "Oh Karl, I love you," over and over again.

I replied, "Oh my darling, I love you too with all my heart."

Here we were, two people who had never even touched each other before, not even by shaking hands. One was a prisoner of war, outside the camp in forbidden territory, and the other, a young English lady. Yet we were in each other's arms in the middle of an English country lane, oblivious to what was going on around us.

I don't know how long we stood there, kissing, hugging, and stroking each other's faces. We heard voices saying, "Hello," and looked up to see a middle-aged couple walking by with a big smile on their faces.

This brought us out of the clouds and Sue greeted them with a "Good afternoon."

Before we walked on, arm in arm, Sue took a handkerchief out of her handbag and wiped the lipstick from my face. Now I remembered the forget-me-nots in my pocket. I took them out and proudly handed them to her. Unfortunately they were a little squashed from all that hugging and squeezing. She said, "Oh how thoughtful of you." Then she put her arms around me again and I was rewarded with another kiss.

We sat down under the big tree. Then we kissed again and Sue wished me a happy birthday. I could not remember a happier birthday in my entire life. Sue opened her handbag and brought out sandwiches, one for each of us, and also some cookies, which her mother wanted us to have. How wonderful it felt to sit so close to her. There she was, sitting at my side, looking at me with her big beautiful eyes, holding and stroking my hand.

So far we had hardly talked, but we had a lot to tell each other. The first thing Sue wanted to know was how old I was. I told her I was 22. She would not tell me her age, however, and kept me guessing for a long time. She was afraid I would think she was too young for me.

After a while, Sue brought out a packet of cigarettes for me. I took one and realized that I had no matches. A few minutes later, a family walked by. The man was smoking, so I saw my chance to get a light. I was about to get up to speak to the man when Sue took hold of my arm and whispered, "Please don't, please don't."

I said, "Don't worry, it will be all right," walked up to the man and said, "Have you a light please?"

He said, "Sure," reached into his pocket for his lighter and lit my cigarette. I then thanked him and bid him a good afternoon and Sue called out to them, wishing them a pleasant day.

As I sat down next to her, Sue said, "You are really daring."

"I wouldn't be sitting here next to you, if I wasn't," I replied.

While I was smoking, Sue started talking, telling me all about her parents and her two sisters, Pat and Daisy. She was just bubbling over. I got to know all the things I had been wondering about, including where they lived. I also got to know about their dog, Sally, and her cousins. She then asked me if I had a photograph of myself. I told her I did and it was all I possessed, but it was taken in my air force uniform. Since I didn't have it with me, I promised I would send it in my next letter.

I told Sue a little about my family and mentioned that a few days

ago I had the first sign of life from them for three years. She could not fully comprehend the devastating circumstances in Germany. I didn't really know myself at the time. Besides many other things, she wanted to know how and where I was taken prisoner. I did not go into details, but gave her a rough idea where and how it happened.

The afternoon went by so quickly. Soon it was 3 o'clock. Sue pointed out that it would take her two hours to get home and she wanted to be there before dark. Her father still didn't know that she was seeing me, and she didn't want him to find out just yet.

I put my arms around her and told her that I wished with all my heart we wouldn't have to leave each other. She said, "Oh Karl, believe me, I don't want to. I would like to stay here with you for all eternity."

We kissed again and Sue whispered, "Karl darling, I have to go."

I gave her another big kiss and held her tight for a few more moments.

We walked down the country lane, away from the big tree, and then stopped to look back at it. I thought to myself, I must remember this tree for the rest of my life. As we walked arm in arm, I told Sue that I would come with her as far as I possibly could. We both grew quiet. The thought of having to part was too painful and I tried to cast it out of my mind.

As we got close enough to see the bus stop, Sue looked at her watch again and said, "We have ten minutes." So that we couldn't be seen by anyone, we stepped into some shrubs and then we were in each other's arms again. I held her so close to me that I could feel her heart beating. Sue kept saying, "Oh Karl, please be careful when you go back, promise you will be careful, I love you so much". We kissed and squeezed and kissed until it was time for her to leave.

Before we let go of each other, I told her once more how much I loved her and said, "One day I will be free, please wait for me. In the meantime I will write to you." I stayed till she was on the bus and riding away.

Slowly I walked back towards the camp. It was still very light, so I lay down in some bushes and fell asleep. When I opened my eyes, it was getting dark. I waited a little longer until it was completely dark and then made my way towards the camp.

When I got there I heard a voice calling, "Come on Karl, it is open." It was Seppie. He had the barbed wire already separated. I crawled through, and was back inside.

19

Heinz was also there with a bundle of clothes under his arms saying, "Quick, get changed, you can't be seen in here in this uniform." He had my clothes ready for me to put on. I was glad they were there, because I had completely forgotten about the uniform that I was wearing. I put the British uniform in a sack, which Seppie held out for me and took back to the kitchen.

Heinz told me I had better go to the washroom and clean my face because I smelled like a lady. Then I remembered that Sue had forgotten to wipe the lipstick off my face. She was too upset to notice when we parted.

Heinz came with me to the washroom. He looked around to make sure we were alone. Then he told me what happened after I left.

First Theo came to tell them that he would be bringing my clothes to them near the fence after dark. All this was fine and no problem. Then, at around 3 o'clock, all the guards went through the barracks, rounding everybody up from the playing field for a camp roll call. They were both really afraid for me. They were almost sure that someone had seen me outside and wondered if I belonged to the camp.

While the guards were counting, Seppie and Heinz were shuffling around from one row to the other, so as to confuse the count. They managed to do this a few times so there were several recounts. Finally, someone came out of the washroom and stood in line, they recounted again, the number was correct and the roll call was over. They did not find out that I was missing.

Theo later told me that the person who came out of the bathroom was none other than himself. Whenever there was a roll call, they always counted the kitchen staff first in their white uniforms. Then they counted the rest of the camp. So after they had counted everybody, he slipped into my POW outfit, sneaked into the washroom, and then came out again and joined the line, making the guards believe he had been there all the time.

I shall never forget that day as long as I live. The next morning I missed Sue more than ever before. I wished that I didn't have to wash away the fragrance of her lipstick from my face. That night I went to sleep hoping that in my dreams I could relive every second of that Sunday afternoon.

The next evening, after returning from the brickyard, I sat down to write a long letter. I had to let Sue know that I made it safely back into the camp. I didn't want her to worry too long, because I knew she would.

The next two weeks were uneventful. I enjoyed the spring flowers in the camp. It made such a big difference to the everyday dull camp life. Since I was still trying to improve my English, I spent a lot of time studying. But each morning my first thought was of Sue. I wished there was a better way of meeting her. I had to find a way to get in and out of the camp more easily.

With this in mind I spent a lot of time the next day near the barbed wire fence. I concentrated on the corner of the camp, where I had been going out before. This area was more sheltered with some bushes outside the camp close to the wire. What I needed to do was to put a permanent hole in the fence and then separate the barbed wire so that I could crawl through it. My friends would have to stay close to me and watch out for anyone approaching while I worked on the fence.

The next Saturday, while most of the boys watched the soccer game, I made my escape hatch with the help of a pair of poultry scissors from Theo. Now all was set for Sue's next visit. Of course, every Saturday and Sunday I never failed to look for Sue coming along the rails to visit me. Since it was impossible for her to write to me, this was the only way.

Almost a month had gone by without a visit from Sue. Then one drizzly Saturday afternoon I saw her approaching the camp. Heinz and Seppie were in the barracks and I was the only one outside in the wet weather.

As she came up to the fence, I called to her that I was coming out. She said, "Oh, no," but before she could say anything else I was already on my way. I looked quickly behind me to make sure no one saw me, crawled through the already prepared opening, and in no time I was outside.

I walked towards the bushes closest to the fence. Sue was still standing next to the barbed wire. For a moment she hesitated, then she came running after me. We stood under her umbrella, hugging and kissing, not realizing that the rain had stopped. Then she gave me a letter, cigarettes, and food. I put them all underneath my jacket.

As Sue folded up her umbrella, I saw a man coming towards us, pointing a pitchfork. I said to Sue, "Quickly go home, I can take care of myself." She started running towards the rails without looking back. As the man came closer I recognized him as the farmer from next door. Knowing that I could not defend myself, I started running. He ran after me, waving his pitchfork.

My first instinct was to run for the opening in the barbed wire, but then I realized I would be giving away my secret. Instead I ran around the meadow. I knew that I could easily outrun him, so I kept on running. Several times he called for me to stop, but the distance between us became greater by the minute.

When the farmer realized he couldn't catch me, he started running towards the guardhouse, and I ran back to the camp. In no time I was crawling through the opening in the fence and heading for the barracks. I climbed into my bunk and covered myself up to my head with my blanket.

It was not long before a guard came into our barracks, looking around. I pretended to be snoring and hoped he would not remove my blanket as my clothes were damp and would have given me away. Finally he left. While the guards checked all the barracks I stayed in my bunk.

Later that evening I went to tell Heinz and Seppie about my unusual experience with the farmer during the afternoon, and to share my cigarettes with them. They found my story very amusing.

Sue's letter was full of memories of that Sunday afternoon. She told me that she was heartsick and lovesick. Her greatest wish was to be close to me and she would wait for me, no matter how long it took.

20

I loved the Yorkshire countryside. All around us were farms. Many times I wished I had a camera to take pictures of the lovely flowers in the camp. My forget-me-nots at the entrance to our barracks were now in full bloom. I hated being cooped up, surrounded by barbed wire.

In my next letter to Sue I suggested that instead of her coming to the camp, I would meet her outside it on a narrow path, which was sheltered by undergrowth and shrubs, some of them up to six feet tall. I told her that it had to be early on a Sunday afternoon. It was risky, but I had to take a chance.

That same evening I told Heinz and Seppie, my faithful guards, of my plan, and as usual they went along with it, although it was almost as daring as going down into the quarry. This had to be done in my POW outfit and in broad daylight.

It was a sunny and warm Sunday when the three of us made our way towards the corner of the camp. The boys were playing soccer as usual. One of the guards was standing among the spectators, watching the game and cheering it on. But he was so involved in the game that I didn't think he would notice what was going on around him.

I positioned myself ready to crawl through the opening, waiting for Heinz and Seppie to let me know when it was a good time for me to go. Soon I got the signal for the OK, and in less than a minute I had slipped through the hole in the barbed wire, and was outside.

I looked around, to make sure all was clear, and then crept down through the fields, taking advantage of every little bit of cover, such as shrubs and tall grass.

A good half an hour went by and I didn't see anyone, not even Sue. I reached the path and looked around for a place where we could be hidden. Now and again I heard the boys cheering the soccer game back at the camp. Eventually I heard some voices close by. Through the bushes I saw a couple with their daughter standing on the path. They were talking to Sue.

Eventually the people walked past me and I called out softly to Sue from my hiding place. Moments later we were in each other's arms, kissing and squeezing each other. For a long time neither of us said anything. We just listened to each other's heartbeat.

We sat down next to each other in the bushes and Sue told me that the people she talked to had stopped her because she was alone. They told her to be careful, walking alone with a German prisoner of war camp so close by. She felt like saying, "That is the reason why I am here." Instead she replied that she was aware of it but it didn't bother her and she was waiting to meet up with some friends.

After a while Sue opened her handbag and brought out cigarettes and sandwiches, and we shared one together. Then she proudly showed me the photo of me in my air force uniform, which I had sent her. She said she loved it and would always carry it with her.

As usual time flew by. The sun was getting lower, but it was becoming more and more difficult for us to part. Several times Sue said, "Please hold me tight, Karl, and don't let me go."

Nevertheless, it was time to go back. Sue had to walk to the bus stop, to be home before dark. I could not walk with her because I was in my POW outfit with the big yellow sun on the back of my jacket.

We embraced once more and kissed passionately. Sue whispered softly in my ear, "I do so love you with all my heart, Karl, I really do."

My heart ached as I watched her walk away but I stayed in the shrubs and waited for it to get dark.

Suddenly I heard loud noises coming from the path. It sounded like a whole family was coming my way. I thought I could remain hidden, but they had a dog, a medium-sized terrier, which picked up my scent and charged towards me.

The more I called to him to go away the more he barked at me. Growling and showing his teeth, he kept jumping up at me. This was serious. If the people found out that I was a prisoner of war, there was no telling what they would do. I could not tell them that I was a Polish volunteer, in my unmistakable POW outfit.

I could probably have made a run for it, but a barking, snarling dog would have alerted the whole camp and all the guards. That was the last thing I wanted.

Before long, the dog's owner came to find out what his dog was barking at so fiercely. Desperate situations call for desperate measures and I did the first thing that came to mind in a situation like this. I pulled down my trousers and sat on my haunches as if I was going to the bathroom. I was just in time. A few seconds later, the dog's owner appeared before me. When he saw me sitting there with my trousers down, he stopped in his tracks and apologized. Then he dragged the dog away, saying to it, "You naughty dog."

With a tremendous sigh of relief I pulled up my trousers and made my way back to the camp. The sun was just setting when I reached the opening in the barbed wire. As I was crawling through I heard Seppie say, "Come in Karl, all is clear."

Later in the evening I read Sue's letter. She mentioned that the police had been to their house. The officer complained that she had been seen fraternizing with a German prisoner of war, which was against the law. Sue was worried in case they knew who the prisoner was. Her mother asked the officer, if he had a son in a German prisoner of war camp, wouldn't he be pleased if someone gave him food? The officer answered, yes he would, but the law was the law, and it was his duty to warn them that if this happened again, there would be serious consequences.

I was equally concerned for Sue. I didn't think that they knew who the prisoner was, otherwise I would surely have heard about it, or have been transferred to another camp.

Before going to sleep that evening I had to write to Sue and tell her about my incredible experience, but I didn't go into details. By this time I was so much in love that I would have done anything, no matter how dangerous, just to be near her.

In the meantime my friend Seppie had put together a camp choir.

They had permission to put on a performance in the camp at some later date, and invite the British public.

My English had improved quite a lot by this time. I kept a book in which I wrote all my German words in black ink, and all my English words in red ink. The summer was coming to an end and there was a whiff of fall in the air in the mornings. Some of the leaves were turning brown, which reminded me of home and the birch trees in their autumn colors. It made me feel rather homesick.

One morning at roll call we were informed that in the near future we would be allowed to send one letter every six months to our families at home. It was the first sign that restrictions were beginning to ease off a little. The letter had to be left open so that it could be censored. Then it had to be sealed and stamped by British personnel. It was certainly a welcome improvement for all of us.

I spent most of my evenings studying. With Christmas only a few months away, I wanted to get some material together to make a few toys. I had already saved some different colored toothbrushes, which I would be using to make cigarette holders. Since we had practically no tools to work with, it would take weeks to make one cigarette holder. We usually got the materials we needed from the civilians we met at work. In our barracks alone, carved birds, pecking on a board, cigarette holders, and fancy slippers were being made. One of our men even built ships inside bottles. I myself was concentrating on making a plastic bracelet, dolls cradles, and cigarette holders.

21

A few weeks had gone by since I last saw Sue. Every Saturday and Sunday I hung around near the barbed wire at the corner of the camp, so that I could see her coming. Today was a beautiful fall day. It was somewhat cool but the sun was out and the country air smelled fresh. I was watching a cat with her three kittens, belonging to a fellow prisoner from the next barracks, playing around a large cardboard box. The farmer he worked for had given them to him. There were other spectators besides myself and it was very entertaining to watch the kittens play. While I walked up and down along the fence, listening to the camp choir practicing, I could hear Seppie singing *Oh solo mio* in his beautiful tenor voice.

Finally I saw two people walking along the railway lines towards the camp, Sue and another girl. I looked behind me to see if anyone was close by. Seppie and Heinz were not around and I did not have much time. It was too late to go and find them so I just had to hope for the best. The thought of seeing Sue again after so many weeks dispelled all fears of being caught so I went as close as I possibly could to the barbed wire.

Sue told me she didn't have much time today and introduced me to her friend, Betty. Then there came flying over the fence a letter, sandwiches, and an envelope with writing paper and postage stamps. The letter disappeared quickly under my jacket. Sue said that she had been ill with an inner ear infection, and that was why she hadn't been to see me sooner.

Suddenly Sue spotted two guards coming our way, and warned me of them. I said, "I love you, darling. You'd better go and be careful." Then I threw the food and the envelope next to me in the grass, hoping the guards wouldn't see me do it.

It was too late for me to get away. They called out, "Stay where you are," and marched me off, one guard in front of me and one behind me, to the guardhouse.

I was taken to the camp sergeant, who asked me, "Do you speak English?" I just shrugged my shoulders. He then called for an interpreter to be brought in, one of our men, and asked if I knew that it was not allowed to fraternize and that I had to keep at least ten feet away from the fence. I asked the interpreter to tell him that I didn't realize I was that close to the fence. He responded by shouting at me that he would like to put on boxing gloves and punch me on the nose.

I couldn't help laughing at that, so he realized that I understood English. This made him even more furious. He jumped up, throwing his desk over in front of me. For a moment I thought he was going to come for my throat. Instead, he threw his arms up in the air and told me that he was going to report this incident to the camp commander. Instead of going to work next day, I would receive my punishment.

Back at the barracks, Heinz and Seppie had already heard that I had been caught and were anxiously waiting to hear what I had to tell them. They said that anyone who was reported to the camp commander received a very severe punishment. Now I really wished that I had taken the time to look for Heinz. He could probably have prevented me from being caught.

I could not change what had happened, so I had to get a letter to Sue quickly. Since I was not allowed to go to work, I was hoping that either Seppie or Heinz would mail a letter for me.

But first the sandwich and the envelope had to be retrieved before nightfall. Luckily, the guards had not seen me throwing them away. Before it was too dark my two friends accompanied me to retrieve everything. While they were on the lookout, I retrieved the items. We moved to a different area to share the food. Then I went to my barracks to read the letter from Sue.

I had to destroy the letter after I had read it, so it would not get into the hands of anyone else. We never knew when the guards would be conducting a search. I was just about to lie down on my bunk when the interpreter came in to tell me that the sergeant wanted to see me again.

As we walked to the guardhouse, the interpreter had some good news for me. The sergeant's wife was visiting him when I was caught. She was Austrian, of German descent, and she wanted to know what had happened at the fence. He told her about me and that he was going to have to make a report to the camp commander. She persuaded him not to report me, but to find another way to deal with the situation.

At the guardhouse the sergeant told me, in a much softer voice, that he had a relative with a son in a German prison camp, and so he had decided not to report me to the camp commander. However, I would have to be taught a lesson. Starting the following day, for seven days, I would be locked in the coal enclosure and spend the day shoveling coal from one side to the other. With this I was dismissed.

Walking back to my barracks, I was immensely relieved. Now I had to get a letter off to Sue to let her know that I was all right. I hoped that Seppie could mail it. He was working for a farmer and hopefully there was a mailbox nearby.

Monday morning came far too soon. Promptly I reported at the guardhouse for my special duty. The coal enclosure consisted of a concrete base, approximately 15 feet square. An eight-foot high chain-link fence surrounded it.

Before the guard on duty locked me inside, he ordered me to take off my shoes and socks, which he kept. He wanted me to be barefoot. Then he handed me a shovel. As he closed and locked the gate behind me, he called out in broken German, "Mack snell, mack snell" [Hurry up, hurry up]. He then went back to the guardhouse, about 20 feet away.

Most of the guards were young soldiers about my age. Every so often, one of them would call through a small window in the guard house, "Mack snell, mack snell."

By the end of the first day I had just about shoveled the whole pile of coal, about ten feet high, from one end of the enclosure to the other. I only got two slices of bread with some water for the whole day. My feet ached, and they were black with coal dust. I was not used to working barefoot, on top of pieces of coal on a cold concrete floor. At dusk, one of the guards let me out, handed me my shoes and socks, and told me to report back the next day.

When I got back to my barracks I was weary, tired, and hungry. Seppie came over to see me and told me that he managed to mail my letter. That kind of news made me feel better.

I went to the washhouse to wash the dirt and coal dust off my sore feet. When I climbed into my bunk at night I felt depressed and hungry. I just lay there feeling sorry for myself. Then I reached for my dictionary and leafed through it, looking for words I wanted to learn. It helped me to take my mind off the unpleasant day I had experienced. I thought of Sue saying, "Oh Karl I will never stop loving you."

Some time later, Heinz came to keep me company and to cheer me up a little. He also brought me a potato, which he had smuggled into the camp and baked for me on the potbelly stove. It was nice and hot and tasted as good as the best steak.

Although I was very tired, I didn't sleep much that first night. I was reliving the moments with Sue on that memorable Sunday afternoon, when I daringly climbed down into the quarry to spend the afternoon with my darling.

In the letter, which Seppie had mailed for me, I asked Sue not to come to the camp for at least two weeks, even though I wanted to see her more than ever. I told her that I was OK and that I had special duties to perform in the camp, but I didn't go into details.

The next day, when I reported to the guardhouse, there was a different guard on duty. He was middle-aged, and to my surprise he did not ask me to remove my shoes and socks before he locked me in the enclosure. Apart from bringing me bread and water, I never saw him all day. Neither did he call out, "mack snell, mack snell". I felt like saying to him, God bless you, you are a good man. But I couldn't bring myself to do it.

As the second day of my special duty came to an end, I did not feel as tired and I was in somewhat better spirits than the day before. Also, I did not re-shovel the whole pile of coal from one end to the other, as on the previous day. I hoped that the same guard would be on duty for the rest of the week.

As the week progressed, I experienced only two more days like that first Monday. Each time, the same young soldier was on duty, ordering me to take my shoes and socks off. However, as the week wore on, I became wiser. When he called through the little window, "Mack snell," instead of actually shoveling coal, I only moved my shovel back and forth, making enough noise that it could be heard in the guardhouse. Once in a while of course, when he came to check up on me, I had to shovel coal. Experience had taught me some survival techniques over the years.

Thinking of Sue, and not being able to hold her in my arms, hurt me more than shoveling coal in my bare feet all day. My heart longed to find a permanent solution. However our love for each other was stronger than the prison camp and the barbed wire, which surrounded it. Maybe it was because of all the obstacles that our love grew so strong.

22

Two weeks after my special duty was over, it was Sunday afternoon again, I was watching for Sue. Both Seppie and Heinz were close by, looking out for me, in case she appeared. This time we wanted to be prepared.

There was no soccer game because it was getting close to Christmas and almost everyone was busy, making toys. I had finished my bracelet for Sue. It was made from clear plastic; the center was heart-shaped with the letters U and K engraved in the middle. I had it in my pocket, ready to give to her if she came. I was feeling uneasy, because of what happened three weeks ago, so I intended to go through the barbed wire as soon as I saw her coming, before she even got close to the camp.

Heinz caught sight of Sue first and as soon as I got the signal I was outside and on my way to the railway lines. Before long we were in each other's arms. As we hugged and kissed I could feel her shaking. She whispered, "Oh Karl, I love you so much and I am so afraid for you."

I reached into my pocket and gave her the bracelet, together with a card I had made. It read '*This is for you dear, please don't open it until you get home.*'

Sue had brought a letter, food, and cigarettes. For a few moments the world around us stood still, but all too soon it was time to part again.

As she turned to go, Sue said, "I love you Karl, please be careful, I don't want anything else to happen to you." I stayed until she was out of sight, then made my way back into the camp on hands and knees. Seppie and Heinz were both relieved when they saw me inside again.

Two weeks later, I was assigned to a different commando, a work site about 20 minutes from where Sue lived. It turned out to be the hardest work I had done so far. We had to dig trenches about six to eight feet deep. Whenever we had dug about ten feet of trench, huge pipes were laid in them, and then it was my job to refill the trench with dirt.

One day, one of the men was working a jackhammer deep down in the trench. We had encountered large rocks, which had to be broken up. While he was hammering and chipping away, his jackhammer slipped. Since it was a very heavy tool, he fell forward and scraped both hands against the rocks. The force of the fall pulled out nearly all his fingernails. The pain was so severe that he ran up an almost vertical wall and out of the trench.

After he was taken to hospital, the foreman picked me to replace him. I tried hard to explain that my wrists and arms were too small and too weak to do work like that. I didn't think I had the strength to even lift the hammer.

However it was no use, I had to go down and operate the jackhammer. As I had thought, I barely managed to lift it up. The trench not only had boulders, but also water, which had seeped through and collected at the bottom. After about five minutes of hammering, I was so weak that I lost control, fell over, and ended up lying in a deep puddle. The foreman who was watching me from the top was furious and called, "Get out of there you stupid fool." As I climbed out of the trench, I said a silent prayer of thanks and then reassumed my original job, filling the trenches with dirt.

That evening I was told to report to the camp sergeant again. With dreadful foreboding I made my way to the guardhouse.

The sergeant behind the desk said in a very official manner, "Your fraternizing behavior has earned you a black mark against your name. Consequently, we have to send you to another camp, far away from here." My heart sank into my boots. I felt like somebody had hit me with a sledgehammer, though I tried hard not to show it. There would be about a hundred of us from nearby camps boarding a train from the city of Leeds, and we would be leaving in about a week's time.

If someone had told me that I was going to face a firing squad, I couldn't have felt any worse. I asked myself, could this now be the end of our romance?

Heinz and Seppie were waiting for me when I got back. They told me that I looked as if I had seen a ghost and were very sorry to hear that I was going to be moved so far away. We had been such good friends. I could trust them as if they were my own brothers.

Seppie suggested I write a letter to Sue and get it in the mail as soon as possible, so there would be time for her to come and see me once more before I left.

I must have sat on my bunk for at least half an hour with my head in my hands, not knowing how to start. It was something I had dreaded for a long time but how was I going to tell Sue that I might never see her again?

Eventually I managed to put a letter together. Now I had to find a way to get it mailed. If only I could find someone who would hand a letter to her personally. Then I remembered that one of the timber-men I used to work with at the Clayton building site had once seen Sue handing a letter to me. She was probably still going to her cousin's house, using the pathway across the building site, at least, I hoped the pathway still existed.

I wrote another letter, asking Sue to come to the camp and see me on the coming Sunday afternoon. I didn't go into details; but said it was very important.

I found my former colleague in his barracks and he said he would be glad to give Sue the letter. I mentioned that the best time to see her would probably be on Friday afternoon around 4:30 p.m. and if by any chance he didn't see her by Friday, would he please destroy the letter.

Seppie and Heinz gave me yet another idea. I should write another note, which they would give to Sue if all else failed and Sue came to the camp after that Sunday. At least she would know that I had been moved away.

On Friday I went to find my friend the timber-man. He had good news for me. He had given Sue the note and furthermore she asked him to tell me that she had also received my letter in the mail. So in spite of my sadness I could at least look forward to seeing her on the coming Sunday.

By Saturday noon I had my few belongings packed, ready to leave. I looked out for Sue, but she didn't turn up.

Sunday turned out to be a nice day. I expected Sue to come early, so around noon I started watching out for her. My two friends soon joined me. The boys were playing soccer, which captured most people's attention and gave me a much better chance to go outside without being seen. After a while, Heinz came to warn me that there was a guard watching the soccer game. So we would have to make sure he was distracted when I went through the wire.

Around mid-afternoon I saw Sue coming towards the camp. Heinz and Seppie created a kind of shield, to hide me while I went through the opening. Then they stood next to each other facing the playing field and I crawled out.

Sue and I rushed into each other's arms. She was sobbing and kissed me passionately. Neither of us could say anything, we just held each other tight.

After a while Sue calmed down a little. She reached into her handbag and gave me a photo of herself, saying, "Please take this with you." I assured her that I would take it with me wherever I went and that I would treasure it for the rest of my life. It was taken in the garden in front of their house. Sue was wearing a coat with tiny tassels on the collar. I asked her for a tassel to keep with her picture as a reminder of our last moments together outside the camp. 52 years later, I still have the photo and the tassel.

We hugged and kissed until Sue said, "Oh Karl, I have to go." We kissed for the last time. Tears were rolling down her face when she finally turned to leave.

I called out to her, "Please remember, I will always love you."

After she had gone, I stood in the same spot for quite some time, collecting myself. Then I remembered to wipe the lipstick from my face, before I went back inside the camp.

My friends were waiting for me. The soccer game was over, so we spent the rest of the evening together, talking about the future. We exchanged addresses, they wished me all the best and then we parted company.

That night, I read the letter Sue had given me. She told me she would never love anyone else and no matter what it took she would wait for me until we could be together again.

I pictured Sue sitting in the bus on her way home with tears in her eyes. Now I knew how much she must really love me. No matter how uncertain the future looked, I had a feeling that we would meet again.

Sawtry, England

23

Next morning at 9:00 a.m. about thirty of us were loaded onto a truck and taken to the train station in Leeds, where another 150 or so fellow prisoners joined us from nearby camps. We would be traveling south, to a destination as yet unknown to us.

We occupied three carriages of a passenger train. Since it was daylight, we could enjoy the beautiful Yorkshire countryside, with its dark dry stone walls, which brought back vivid memories of our mailbox at the Clayton building site, the walkway and the little bridge. The past 19 months seemed like a dream that had come to an abrupt end.

I noticed the color of the stone walls changing from dark to white and knew that we had left Yorkshire behind and were now in the county of Derbyshire. My foreman Bill once told me that without looking at a map you could tell by the cream-colored walls when you were in Derbyshire.

Although I loved seeing the country, my thoughts were with Sue. I looked at the picture she had given me for a long time. It made me wish she were sitting next to me. So before I started feeling too sorry for myself, I struck up a conversation with the man sitting next to me.

He came from a camp near York. He told me that he thought he was being moved away because he had become friendly with the farmer's daughter at the commando where he had worked. The farmer didn't like that, so he sent a letter to the camp commander, asking for him to be taken off the commando.

I wondered how many more were on this train for similar reasons, and if our camp was going to be specially guarded, or if there were no

Typical Yorkshire Landscape

work commandos.

One of the guards came walking through the carriage. I plucked up the courage to ask him where we were going. He said Peterborough, about 160 miles from the camp in Yorkshire. We would arrive there early the next morning.

It turned out to be a long night for me. I even found myself thinking that it might have been better if Sue and I had never met. But I quickly dismissed that thought. Everything had worked out well so far. It must have been meant to happen.

I fell asleep for a while. When I woke up I felt hungry and thirsty and I had no idea how far we had traveled. Most of my fellow prisoners were asleep. Although the carriages were filled to capacity, I felt alone and a little homesick.

Somewhere during the night the train came to a halt. Our carriages were moved to another rail, where we got off and stood in line for some food and tea, provided by an army canteen. Not long afterwards, we were hooked up again and the journey south continued. I felt much better with food inside me and fell asleep again. When I awoke it was daylight.

We rolled into the city of Peterborough, where we got off the train and boarded three large army trucks. The trip continued to our new camp on Wood Walton Lane, Sawtry, near Connington in the county of Huntingdonshire.

As we were unloaded and went through the large main gates, I could see that it was a very large camp. What surprised me more than anything was the fact that there was no barbed wire. A very high chain-link fence was all that surrounded the camp. Neither did I see any guard towers. The buildings were wooden barracks. I was pleasantly surprised by the relaxed atmosphere. It reminded me more of a regular army camp than a place holding prisoners of war.

Once inside, the gates closed behind us and we had to line up to be individually searched and questioned. I was looked over by a captain. First he found my photo of Sue and wanted to know who she was. I told him she was a longtime friend. Then he wanted to know how I came to be in possession of the photo. I replied that they let me keep it when I was taken prisoner. He looked doubtful, but after a little hesitation he handed it back to me. He also found the folder in which I kept all my English papers. Besides that, all I possessed was a toothbrush, toothpaste and my most treasured English-German dictionary.

After having a good look at my folder, the captain asked me to describe our train ride from Leeds to Peterborough. I was puzzled but told him as well as I could about the countryside and the different landscapes in Yorkshire and in Derbyshire. I later found out that he really wanted to know how well I could speak English. After he was finished, he asked me for my name and wrote it in his notebook.

We next had to wait in line to be interviewed. There was a row of tables set up, behind each of which sat a German prisoner of war. When my turn came, I was asked my name, rank, home address, and religion. The man behind the table then wrote everything down.

Then something very unusual happened. The man who sat at the next table got up, came over to me, and told me that he came from the city of Betzingen, which was no more than five miles from where I grew up. He also belonged to the same church as me and it turned out that we had attended confirmation class together. What a small world! There we were, over a thousand miles from home, and I meet a man who sat with me in confirmation class so many years before.

He asked me to come and visit him in his barracks as soon as we were through and pointed to a small hut in the middle of the camp.

The barracks were very similar to those at the Westfield camp. They were wooden and had a potbelly stove in the middle. However, they were larger, accommodating about 80 of us. This time I had the bottom bunk. All the men in our barracks were from the Yorkshire area and we were all new arrivals.

That same evening I went to look for the small hut, standing all by itself in the middle of the camp. My new friend, who was called Helmut Haas, lived there all by himself because he was the mail orderly of the camp. He also took care of a book in which he had to record all the punishments for the whole camp. Every incident had to be registered. As far as the mail was concerned, every one was allowed to send a letter to Germany once every six months. It was his job to collect the letters and take them to be censored. Also, first thing in the morning, it was his duty to go up to the British office and collect all the incoming mail, which he had to distribute to the respective British personnel and all the prisoners of war.

All the prisoners were classed as either 'A' (which stood for 'anti-

Nazi'), or 'B' (which stood for 'in between'). 'C' stood for 'Nazi'. There were no 'C' classifications allowed in this camp.

That must be why there were no guard towers or barbed wire around the camp, only a tall fence. It had no political problems. Helmut told me that every week about 50 men from the 'A' category were repatriated back to Germany and then replaced by men from other camps around the country. We, the men who were sent here from Yorkshire, must be classified either 'A' or 'B'. I later found out that my classification was 'B' because I had belonged to the '*Jung Volk*' but was not a Nazi sympathizer.

My new friend confirmed my suspicion that many of the men who were sent away to another camp had been caught fraternizing. He then asked me if I could speak English. I said, yes I could, and mentioned that the captain who interviewed me asked me questions about the trip down here. Helmut explained that they were looking for a replacement for him to take care of the mail because he would be repatriated home in a month's time.

Helmut had dealings every day with the captain who interviewed me. He promised me that first thing next day he would tell him that he thought I was the perfect replacement for him.

We talked for almost two hours. I told him all about the girl I knew from Yorkshire and our meetings outside the camp. He thought we should definitely keep up our relationship and he would see to it that we could continue to communicate with one another. In fact, he insisted I write a letter to Sue as soon as possible. Since it was his job to collect the mail every morning, he would look through it and take out the letters addressed to me. She could even send a parcel because he would make sure I received it. My heart leaped with joy at these exciting possibilities.

Before I left, Helmut made me a cup of coffee. I was amazed at the privileges he had as a mail orderly. When I got back to my barracks everyone was busy introducing themselves. Some were familiarizing themselves with the layout of the camp.

I myself looked for a quiet place where I could write a letter to Sue. First I lay down on my bunk so that I could collect my thoughts. I felt almost as if I were in a dream. When I finally got up to write I realized that I hadn't any writing paper. The only solution I could think of was to go back and ask Helmut if he could lend me some.

I went to his hut and found him busy making entries in a book. He had writing paper and envelopes and suggested I sit down right there to write, so I would not be disturbed.

I wrote Sue a long letter. There was so much to tell her. Helmut kept my letter so he could mail it for me first thing the next morning.

It was getting late. The man on the top bunk wanted to know where I had been all evening. I told him that I had met an old friend from back home and we had a lot to tell each other. Soon afterwards the lights were switched off and I was fast asleep.

The following day was more or less uneventful. I found out that many of my fellow prisoners were working; most of them were on farm commandos, and many on road works and various building projects. I walked all around the camp and was amazed how large it was. What surprised me more than anything was that there was absolutely no barbed wire to be seen anywhere. Of course there was a soccer field and I noticed some cats. It looked like quite a few of the men kept pets.

I needed a haircut so I looked up the barbershop. That was usually the place where all the rumors started. The barber confirmed that there were repatriations almost every week. He knew Helmut, the mail orderly, and had heard a whisper that Helmut would be repatriated in a few weeks time.

As I walked by the camp entrance I saw some trucks dropping off men who had come back from their work commandos. That meant it must be close to 5 o'clock and I wondered what was on the menu for supper. As it turned out we got two slices of white bread and a kind of watery pea soup, much better than what we had at the other camp. I missed the sandwiches and cigarettes, which Sue used to bring me. Above all I missed Sue.

I didn't want to bother Helmut too much so I decided to wait until he contacted me. With a camp of that size he would have his hands full taking care of the mail for everyone. He had mentioned that some days it took him all evening to get everything done.

Later that evening I was sitting on my bunk teaching myself some more English when Helmut walked into my barracks looking for me. He told me that the captain had one other potential candidate for his job and that he would interview both of us. My interview was to be in three days time, at 9:0 a.m. in Helmut's office.

He thought there was a good chance that I would get his job. The captain would make a decision the day I was interviewed because the new orderly had only three weeks to be trained.

24

Three days after we had arrived at the camp, a man whom I didn't know came into our barracks asking for Karl Kern. I introduced myself and he handed me an envelope addressed to me. It was in Sue's handwriting and I could not figure out how a letter from her could end up here so soon after we had left Yorkshire.

I asked the man to sit down and tell me how it came about. He explained that when my group arrived at the camp, it was discovered that there were two men with the 'C' classification. They were sent back to Yorkshire and two others with a 'B' classification were sent in their place. He was one of those two men and he had worked with Seppie for a time. When Seppie heard that the man was coming here he immediately thought of Sue. The same day he asked my former workmate, the timber-man, to tell Sue to write a letter to me by the next day, and he would have it delivered to me.

All the parties involved agreed to help out and the man carried the letter in his shoe all the way here. I was so grateful to him for what he did. I could only hope to be able to do something for him in return some day.

I couldn't wait to read my letter, so I just turned sideways in my bunk and started reading. There were quite a few pages. Sue told me about the timber-man approaching her and how she wasn't sure if he was genuine. But he seemed serious, and he knew Seppie, so she had complied.

She also told me how heartbroken she was in the bus on her way home, after we had said our last good-byes. Her mother was very concerned about her, and had told her father about our relationship. He was somewhat taken aback, but remarked that if his daughter really loved me there was nothing he could do anyway, and she had his blessing.

Sue reassured me that she loved me with all her heart and no matter how long it took, she was willing to wait for me. Reading her letter made me feel very lovesick and I hoped that she would soon receive my letter.

The following morning I rose early. I felt that my continued relationship with Sue depended entirely on the outcome of my interview. There was nothing I could do to prepare myself, so I just hoped and prayed that my English would be good enough.

Promptly at 9 o'clock I knocked at Helmut's door. I learned that the interview with the other candidate did not go very well. His English was not as good as they expected.

When the captain arrived the result seemed to be a foregone conclusion. He wanted to know how Helmut and I knew each other. I explained the circumstances and he simply outlined some of the new duties which were expected of the mail orderly and then told me that I would be working with a lance corporal who would oversee my work and keep me informed of any new rules concerning mail. He would also be escorting me to the post office or anywhere else it was necessary for me to go outside the camp. With this the interview was over. The captain mentioned that Helmut would be repatriated soon and that he should start teaching me immediately. He also wished me well in my new assignment.

As soon as the door closed behind him Helmut said, "This calls for a celebration." We had a cup of coffee together, and a piece of raisin cake, which he had saved for the occasion.

For the next three weeks I spent every day with Helmut, accompanying him every morning to pick up the mail, and learning how to sort it and where to deliver the mail belonging to the British personnel.

One morning, about a week later, Helmut picked up a letter and said, "Do you recognize this handwriting?" Sure enough, it was from Sue. He said, "See how easy it is, just put it in your top pocket and everything is fine."

Sue mentioned in her letter that she had sent me a parcel. She finished with the initials BOLTOP and ITALY, which meant *I truly always love you.*

That same day I wrote another letter to Sue, I couldn't wait to tell her that I was going to be the camp mail orderly.

I met with Jack, the lance corporal who was assigned to work with me. He was very tall and very good-natured. As soon as he introduced himself to me, he offered me a cigarette. He said that any time I needed him I just had to look him up. The quarters of the British guards were located in a separate compound within the camp. He took me there so that he could show me where he lived.

Their barracks were similar to ours but a lot smaller. They had single wooden beds, instead of double bunks, and there were six beds in one barrack. He introduced me to two of his fellow guards who were there at the time. One of them was the sergeant in charge of the kitchen. The other was the driver to the captain and the camp commander. He also pointed out to me a small barrack, which was occupied by two of my fellow prisoners. They were the interpreters of the camp.

Eventually I got to know everything to do with the mail as well as how to record all the punishments which were given to offenders. They ranged from stealing firewood from the British personnel to being caught entering the camp with stolen goods from employers.

I learned that the camp commander, who had the rank of colonel, was very severe in his punishments for very minor offenses.

Besides being mail orderly, I was also assistant interpreter. That meant, whenever neither of the interpreters were available, I had to fill in for them. So one evening I was asked to accompany the colonel on a camp inspection.

I could hardly believe my eyes. He asked the sergeant, who also accompanied him, to slice open a tube of toothpaste with a knife, to see if there was anything hidden inside. On another occasion he asked one of our men to empty out his entire straw sack in the middle of the barracks in case he had something hidden there.

A friend of mine whose name was George was a sort of butler to one of the officers. One day the colonel walked into his room and caught George sweeping crumbs from the table with a brush, which was normally used to sweep the floor. George's punishment was to stay barefoot in a tent for one week, without anything to lie on during the night. The bottom part of his tent was rolled up, so that his feet and legs could be seen at all times. He was also required to run continuously. For food he received only a little bread and water.

On another occasion a young man, whose turn it was to keep the fire going in the stove during the winter, was caught taking a piece of wood from the British compound. He received the same punishment.

I had to record these and many more punishments in a book that was kept in my office. Needless to say, the commander was not liked among the British staff because he treated them in a similar way. Among my fellow prisoners he was hated.

Helmut was with me when we picked up Sue's parcel. He put it in an empty mail delivery sack, which he carried to his place, while I delivered the rest of the mail to the British personnel. When I got back, he was as eager as me to see what Sue had sent. The first thing I saw was a Christmas card. We were reminded that Christmas was just around the corner. Then came some cigarettes, a bar of chocolate, and quite a few home-baked Christmas cookies. There were also postage stamps and writing paper. In a separate envelope was a photo of Sue, taken in their front garden with three tiny puppies in her arms.

I shared the chocolate and cigarettes with Helmut. He made a nice cup of coffee and we celebrated my new position as mail orderly, as well as his going home. We then hid the rest of the goodies behind a stack of papers in his office. You never knew, he said, when the commander would make an inspection.

The time came for Helmut to say goodbye. He was carrying a small sack with his very few belongings. I wished him all the best and told him that I would look him up as soon as I was repatriated. I thanked him again for helping me to get this position and he promised that he would pay my family a visit as soon as he got back home.

I went to my barracks to pick up the few items I called my own and moved into the post office, as it was called. The first night felt very strange sleeping in a place all by myself, but it didn't take long to get used to it.

I had one week to write a combined Christmas and birthday card for Sue. Her birthday was on December 22nd. Drawing had always been one of my favorite pastimes, so I drew my own birthday card and added Christmas greetings to Sue, her parents and to her sisters Pat and Daisy.

The winter turned out to be very cold. The biggest problem I had was keeping the fire going in the stove. In the large barracks the men took turns in keeping the stove burning, whereas I had to light it every day myself.

However, I was very fortunate, if I needed extra blankets to keep me warm, all I had to do was ask the lance corporal. He would get me almost anything I asked for. We had already become good friends. I also got to know the kitchen staff.

Once in a while, when I felt cold, I would walk into the kitchen and be given a hot cup of Bovril or coffee. More than once, they also offered me a fried egg and bread for breakfast. They took good care of me, and I never needed to feel hungry again. Considering that I was a prisoner of war, I had it very good. The only thing I missed was my darling Sue. During the nights, as well as in the day, I relived the moments when we were in each other's arms outside the camp.

25

Christmas 1946 came and went without any celebrating. If it hadn't been for the fact that none of the commandos were picked up for work for two days, most of us wouldn't have known that it was the Christmas holidays.

In 1947 regulations began to be lifted. From March onward, all prisoners were allowed to send a letter every month. The camp was subdivided into four sections and each section had a certain time frame in which to write their letters. That way we didn't have to deal with nearly two thousand letters at one time. We were also allowed to send a parcel twice a year.

From the beginning of May, everyone except those who were under some kind of punishment could apply for a pass to go outside the camp within a radius of five miles. This was allowed one weekend a month. However, if anyone disobeyed the rules, he would be severely punished.

At the beginning of March I had to notify one person from each barrack to line up in front of the main gate with the open letters. The captain arrived with two interpreters, a sergeant, and the lance corporal, who was assigned to assist me. One by one the letters were examined. Out of about 500 letters, 15 of them had to be read and interpreted to the captain. I then took the letters to my office. In the presence of the lance corporal I had to seal and stamp them. It took all evening until we were finally finished.

The lance corporal told me that he would pick me up the next day to deliver the mail. The same procedure had to be repeated three times before the letters for the entire camp had been censored and mailed. It was easy for me to add my letter to those that had already been censored.

The next morning around 9:0 a.m., Jack pulled up outside my office in his Land Rover and greeted me with a cheery "Good morning". I had the letters neatly packed in boxes. He helped me load them and we drove to the post office in Connington. We unloaded our boxes and waited in line. At the counter Jack introduced me as the new mail orderly.

The man behind the counter said, "I am Ken, pleased to meet you." He took our mail into a back room and ten minutes later he returned with a slip, verifying that we had delivered 524 letters. The slip was stamped and signed by him.

We drove back to the camp a different way. On the outskirts of the village we stopped outside a house. Jack said, "My girlfriend's house. Just wait, I won't be long." I watched him going up to the house and a young lady opening the door to him. He then glanced back at me and went inside.

While I was waiting, I enjoyed the beautiful countryside. Everything was lush and green. There were flowering hedges, daisies, and daffodils everywhere. Across the road, crocuses were growing all over a large field with cows grazing among them. Then I noticed a small stream running along the side of the road. I recognized watercress growing at the edge of the stream and I got out to gather a good bunch. That would be delicious in a sandwich. Then I noticed some horseradish, so I gathered a nice big bunch of that too.

I sat in the Land Rover, dreaming of the previous spring when I climbed down into the quarry to meet with Sue and hold her in my arms.

Half an hour later we were on our way back to the camp. Jack pulled up in front of the kitchen. As he got out he motioned me to follow him inside. It was close to noon and the cook made us both a sandwich – mine was corned beef with freshly picked watercress in it – and a nice cup of tea to wash it down. Delicious. It reminded me of my younger days when my brother and I used to pick watercress from the stream for my mother.

Next morning when I picked up the mail, I found two letters addressed to me, one from Sue, and the other one from my friend Helmut. I couldn't deliver the mail fast enough to get back to my office and read Sue's letter. She reassured me of her love for me and that she would give anything to be able to see me. She also admitted that on that afternoon, a year ago, she could feel we were meant for each other.

Helmut was very interested to know if Sue still wrote to me. He mentioned that he had recently read an article in the German newspaper, which claimed that an English girl had married a German POW. They were married in a church. He even enclosed a picture of the happy couple, which he had cut out for me. He firmly believed that this would eventually be made legal in England. This was certainly an interesting development.

Helmut also told me about the situation in Germany. A lot of people were going hungry. Many a mother could be seen begging for food in the streets to feed her children. Helmut was still looking for work but his wife and his family were all right. Unfortunately he had not been able to visit my family as yet. He asked me, when we were allowed to send a parcel to Germany, to send flour, soap, and corned beef. These three items were in short supply. He also wanted me to send him flints for cigarette lighters.

Life was becoming better for us POWs. For example, if a farmer wanted to hire POWs to work for him, he could apply for permission for them to live with him. Whoever entered an agreement like that would have to stay with the farmer for a minimum of two years, regardless of when his repatriation came due. Quite a few of the men in our camp had signed up for that, especially those who had had no sign of life from their family at home.

A few days before my birthday I received a beautiful birthday card from Sue. The whole family had signed it. She also told me to look out for a parcel, which gave me something to look forward to.

In the meantime I had made a lot of friends among the British and also the German staff, including the camp doctor, a captain by rank, and the quartermaster, who was a staff sergeant. Among the German POWs there were the driver for the commander, two interpreters, a dentist, some tailors, and four medics who took care of general health complaints and of bandages needed for injuries etc. We had a fairly large staff of German kitchen personnel who cooked for close to 2000 men. I also became very friendly with the British kitchen staff. Because of my dark hair and complexion they called me the 'little Italian'.

I also made friends with some locals. The Pettifers lived about two houses down from the post office in Connington. I got to know them when I met their 17-year-old daughter in the post office. Later I got to know the whole family. They were wonderful people. Mr. Pettifer was one of England's well-known roof thatchers who put straw roofs on cottages, a highly specialized job.

In April I turned 23 and spent my third birthday in captivity. When I was first captured on the first of April 1945, I would never have dreamed that I would still be in England three years later.

Sue sent me a large parcel with all sorts of goodies, including cigarettes and the usual writing materials. She wanted to be sure I had enough writing paper and envelopes. I was beginning to miss her more than anything. Sue told me that some nights she cried herself to sleep because she missed me so much. She assured me that even though we were miles apart, she would somehow find a way to see me at the Peterborough camp. This time she ended her letter with 'HOLLAND', which stands for *hope our love lives and never dies*.

Around 2:00 a.m. someone knocked at the door of my hut. Sleepily, I got up and opened the door. A strange man was standing there, wearing a hat, a trench coat, and carrying a briefcase. He motioned me to be quiet and in a very quiet voice he asked if he could come in. He said one of the guards had told him to come and see me, so reluctantly I invited him inside.

He introduced himself as a member of a group, which looked into acts of cruelty against German prisoners of war. He had heard that our commander ordered cruel punishments for very minor offenses and he needed proof to be able to remove him from his post. He said that he realized this was an unusual request but without my cooperation they could do nothing. He needed to see the punishment register, which I kept. His group was in contact with the British military high command.

At first I hesitated, then I decided that I had to trust him, so I showed him the logbook in which I entered all the punishments. To my surprise he took a camera from his briefcase and proceeded to take pictures of all the pages going back about two years.

After he had finished, he thanked me for helping him and said that he hoped they would be able to relieve the colonel of his command very soon, he felt he had enough evidence.

I could not go back to sleep after he left, I was so worried about the whole incident, especially if he had been sent by the commander, to trap me.

When I delivered my mail to the guardhouse next morning, I spoke with the guard who the man claimed had sent him. He said that he would have come with him, but he dared not leave his post, as he had been all by himself. I was relieved to know it was not a set-up.

May was a busy month for me. Most of us were allowed to apply for a pass to leave the camp and move freely within a radius of five miles at the weekend. We were also allowed to send one parcel to Germany. Each parcel had to be presented in open condition for inspection by an officer.

It was decided that about fifty parcels would be accepted at one time. This meant that it would take almost a month for all the parcels to be taken care of, one barrack at a time. However, there was no room in my tiny office to address, wrap and seal so many parcels.

At the next opportunity I told the lance corporal about my concerns, and he spoke to the captain. It was decided to move the post office and me into a Nissen hut. A few days later, Jack drove me there to have a look.

It was just outside the main gate and was divided into two rooms. One side of it served as the living quarters for me, and the post office was next door. Each half had its own entrance and a window facing the main gate. In the post office were four large tables and a smaller one in the corner, which was to be my desk. There was also a chair. I was very happy with this new arrangement. It was a lot better than I had ever imagined.

On our way back to the camp we again made a detour towards the house of Jack's lady friend. Before he went into the house he told me that he would probably be a little longer than usual. I assured him that I had plenty of time.

I sat alone in the Land Rover for an hour, enjoying the beautiful nature around me. Flowers bloomed in profusion. The whole air was filled with fragrance and I was reminded of my youth.

I used to love roaming the fields around our village. I spent a lot of time on my favorite mountain, Achalm with a shepherd who liked my company. He used to point out to me the plants, which were good to eat. One of them was sour clover that was very tasty and good for quenching one's thirst. Another one was silver thistle. He showed me how to cut away the flower to get to the juicy part underneath.

It was good to forget for a while that I was a prisoner of war. I wondered how much longer they were going to keep us in England. Personally I could not complain about the way I was treated. I enjoyed being mail orderly and I did not go hungry any more, but I didn't like

Eningen-unter-Achalm

being kept behind a wire fence, away from my family and friends.

However I was very thankful that I was well. Many of my fellow compatriots had lost legs and arms or were incapacitated for the rest of their lives. Some of the men in our camp did not know what they would find when they returned home. At least I knew that my family was all right and that I had a home to go to.

I liked listening to the meadowlarks, which nested in the fields around me. I dreamed of my sweetheart whispering, "I will wait for you my darling." The words that I wrote at the bottom of the picture which Sue gave me, echoed in my heart, *And like a miracle come true, I will find my lovely world, and you.*

My dreaming was suddenly interrupted when I heard the door of the house open. I would have enjoyed sitting in the Land Rover all afternoon. On our way back to the camp I asked Jack if he had a photo of his young lady. He stopped the vehicle and proudly showed me a picture of her. He said that they planned to become engaged in the coming fall, and asked me if I had a girlfriend in Germany. I answered that I had a girlfriend but did not tell him where. I felt like telling him the whole story, but decided to put it off till a later date.

Back at the camp, we had an egg sandwich and coffee for lunch and then I made some notes on how I could best organize the inspecting of the parcels. I wanted it to go smoothly and with as little work as possible for me.

It took several trips in Jack's small Land Rover before we had finally moved everything into my own little quarters. The two interpreters and the camp commander's driver lived in the Nissen hut next door to me and I was glad that I was not the only one living in the British compound.

... — and like a miracle
come true —
I will find my lovely world, and you " .... —..

26

That evening I felt like the king of my own castle. Being able to live in the British compound made me feel more secure. The two interpreters from next door paid me a visit. Our conversation was very interesting and I learned a lot. They told me that the camp commander was being replaced during the coming week. I thought it best not to tell them about my encounter that night at 2:00 a.m. I also found out that the three of us would be allowed to use the same kitchen, which supplied the British personnel.

During the next few days I spent much of my time organizing the post office. I wanted to be ready for the big rush of parcels. One afternoon the German camp commander came to see me. With all the new rules and regulations we had to work together a lot and we became good friends.

The day came to collect the first lot of parcels. 50 of our men were lined up in front of my old quarters with their parcels laid open on the ground. Before the British personnel arrived, I made a rough check of the contents and that they all had string and wrapping paper which was properly addressed.

Then Jack, the captain, the sergeant, and two lance corporals arrived. The parcels consisted mainly of flour and sugar, which were very hard to come by in Germany. Those who worked in the mills could purchase the products from their employers. I was happy to have this job but was not looking forward to all the extra work.

Jack and I loaded the parcels into his jeep and took them to my post office. It was not until the early morning hours that I was finished repacking them. When I finally went to bed, I was hoping that Jack would not turn up too early to go with me to the village post office.

The next morning I went into the post office to check up on the mail. To my dismay I found flour and sugar all over the floor. It looked like the work of an animal. Many of the parcels had a hole chewed right through the paper wrapping, exactly were the flour was. I remembered that I once saw a rat when I delivered mail at the Connington post office. It was by a very slow-running stream, which ran through the middle of the village.

When Jack arrived we both looked for an opening, where a rat could have come in, but we found nothing.

Jack suggested we try some rat poison, but I was not too keen on that, so I suggested putting the parcels on the tables. By now it was time for lunch. Jack suggested we go to the canteen, and then after lunch he would help me rewrap all the parcels, which had been eaten into.

It took the rest of the afternoon to rewrap the damaged parcels. We had to discard all the flour the rat had eaten into, which meant that some parcels had hardly anything left in them by the time we had finished. It was too late to go to the village post office before it closed, so we had no choice but to keep the mail for another night. We piled everything up on the tables in the hope that the rat couldn't get at them there.

The next morning I noticed that one of the parcels had a hole eaten into it again. The rat had managed to get onto the table. I rewrapped it, and Jack and I took the parcels to the post office.

Ken wondered why some of the parcels were so small and I explained what had happened. He mentioned that they had experienced problems with rats also. He thought it was because some people put rubbish and bits of food into the brook.

In May a lot of our men applied for passes to leave the camp at the weekend. So far, I had been so busy at the weekends that I hadn't had a chance to go out. In any case I lived in the British camp compound, so I did not need a pass. I was free to come and go whenever I had the time.

It was a cool but beautiful day in May 1947 when I made my first steps outside the gate one Sunday morning. I felt an awful sense of insecurity. Something inside me wanted to make sure I was not seen. For nearly an hour I had to keep telling myself that I was allowed to do this and no one was going to report me. But what if I met someone who didn't know we were allowed to go outside the camp? Then I remembered that about a month earlier it was written in all the newspapers that the

German prisoners of war had received permission to leave the camp unguarded.

When I came to a field full of flowers I sat down to soak in the scenery and enjoy the fragrance of spring to its fullest. I felt a little homesick and wished with all my heart that Sue could share this beautiful Sunday with me. It had been a long time since we had seen each other.

Judging by the sun, it must have been around noontime. I lay down amongst the flowers and fell asleep for an hour or so. When I opened my eyes I saw a farmer walking by with his dog. We greeted each other with, "Good afternoon," and he walked on. How different, I thought, from the time when the other farmer had chased me all over the field with a pitchfork.

As the afternoon progressed, I began to feel more at ease. I was no longer afraid of being seen. As so often when I had time for myself I thought of my homeland and my family and wondered how they were doing. I was concerned about my father, who had some health problems after my mother passed away.

I was feeling hungry. I decided to walk into the village of Connington, which was no more than a 20-minute walk from where I now lived.

On my stroll through the village I met some of my fellow prisoners who had a pass to go out. Walking by the Pettifer's house, I saw their daughter Marjory in the garden. I stopped to say hello. We talked for a while and then her mother came out of the house and invited me in to share a cup of tea with them. I told her I would love to.

I was a little nervous at first but enjoyed the luxury of being in an English home. The conversation was mainly about Germany and me. I told them a little of how I met Sue. Mrs. Pettifer then said without hesitation that Sue would be welcome to stay with them when she came to visit me. I thanked them very much and went on my way.

On my way back to the Nissen hut I noticed a small brook by the roadside with watercress growing there. I picked some and went straight to the canteen, where the cook had some bangers and mash [sausage and mashed potatoes] left over from lunchtime. It tasted good.

The next morning I had another letter from Sue. She mentioned that her father was planning a vacation to the northeast coast of Yorkshire, a place called Sands End. She was hoping to persuade him to go south first, to pay me a visit. It would mean a detour of nearly 300 miles. I was thrilled that there was a slim chance of seeing her and the rest of the family.

Two days later we had the next batch of parcels checked out and Jack helped me take them to my office. I was busy wrapping them until well after midnight. Then I wrote a letter to Sue, to tell her all the news.

About half way through my letter, I heard noises above me in the roof. I could hear the rat make its way towards the front of the Nissen hut and slide down the wall. Then I saw a cloud of dust come out of a hole next to the front wall, followed by a huge rat. In the meantime I had armed myself with a piece of wood, which was left over from winter. I threw it at the rat, but missed, and the rat was gone. I put down some poison and stuffed some old rags into the opening in the wall.

The next day and the day after, the parcels had been eaten into again. It seemed like I had my work cut out for me.

One morning, after coming back from breakfast, I found a dog sitting in front of the door to my Nissen hut. He was a straggly gray mongrel. There was no collar round his neck to identify him. Several times I pushed him away saying, "Go home boy, go home." He just wagged his tail and came back. I decided that the dog must be hungry. Since I knew what it was like to be hungry, I went over to the kitchen to ask the cook for some leftovers for a dog which was sitting outside my door.

I went back to the dog with quite a lot of scraps. When he smelled the food, he jumped up at me with his tail wagging. Watching him eat reminded me of the time when the farmer brought us a plate full of sausages. The dog consumed the food as quickly as we consumed those sausages. I found an old dish and gave him some water to drink. Afterwards I told him to go home and he walked away. I assumed he belonged to one of the nearby farmers, and went about my business.

The next morning the dog was sitting outside my door again. I told him to go home. I went into the post office and tried to close the door behind me, but the dog followed me in. I thought it wouldn't hurt to let him stay; he would be company for me.

The dog went straight to the corner where the rat had landed two nights before. He seemed very excited and started sniffing around. It suddenly occurred to me that if the dog were kept in the post office while we had all those parcels, he would probably keep the rat away. It might be the answer to all our problems.

I told Jack about my idea and he said we could not keep a dog without the commander's permission. He suggested we collect a few parcels and put them in the post office for the rat to have a go at them. Then we could let the commander see the evidence for himself. I thought that was an excellent plan, so I went to let our German commander know that he could schedule ten parcels to be sent the next day.

In the meantime, I had to keep the dog out of the way so I kept him at my place. He felt right at home there and settled down at the foot of my bed.

After one night there were holes in the parcels and flour strewn everywhere. Jack went to bring the commander to my office. When he saw the mess he admitted we had a problem and asked to see the dog. I went next door to fetch him. He took one look at him and said, "This is a wire-haired terrier and known to be a rat catcher, go ahead and keep him."

I was now a camp mail orderly and a dog owner. I had to give him a name. He was kind of straggly, so I thought the name Struppie would suit him. I found a thick piece of string, made a make-shift collar, tied the string to it and said, "Come on Struppie, you and I are going for a walk."

The weather was nice and warm. I decided to take a walk to Connington. As we approached the small brook that winds between the houses, Struppie started acting strange and tried to pull me along. At the end of the village, where everything turned into farmland, I untied him and let him go. I wanted to find out if he would walk with me. We were still following the brook. He ran ahead, but came back when I called him. It appeared that whoever owned him must have trained him.

After a while Struppie stopped and raised his front right leg and sort of bent it like a horse does. He stood there on three legs, sniffing the air. All of a sudden, he charged with tremendous speed down to the brook. I called him to stop but he kept on going. The next thing I knew, he had pulled a rat out of a hole in the embankment. There was a squeal and he bit the creature's neck. He left the rat and ran back to me, wagging his tail. I had to tell him he was a good boy and he went on walking by my side as if nothing had happened.

So I really had adopted a rat catcher, as the Commander said. I thought it best to put him on the rope, because I didn't want him to repeat the performance while we were in the village.

Word got around that I had a dog living with me. One of the cooks had already saved some food for me to give him. Since I did not have any parcels in the post office for the moment, I kept Struppie in my room. It did not take long for him to get used to his new name and he was very good company for me.

The only problem was that he was dirty. I took him with me into the shower. He didn't like the water running over him and growled at me. However I made him stay underneath and gave him a good scrubbing with soap, which made him smell much better.

Two days later I had about 20 parcels ready to go to the post office. That night was going to be the real test for Struppie. When I left the office after work to go next door to my room, he wanted to come with me. However I told him to stay and watch for the rat.

I sat down to write a letter to Sue and everything was very quiet. Suddenly I heard a terrible scream coming from the post office. I ran to see what the commotion was all about and saw that Struppie had caught the rat, bitten its neck, and left it there on the floor. He was wagging his tail and waiting to be praised for it.

Since I didn't know if this was the only rat living in the roof of my Nissen hut, I left Struppie in the post office, much against his wishes. With 20 parcels sitting there, I didn't want to take any chances. However, there wasn't a sound to be heard all night, and when I came to check the next morning, everything was fine.

I had no more problems with rats from that day on.

27

The next day I received another letter from Sue. She said her father was planning to come to Connington by car some time in July and they would stay for about three days at a nearby bed and breakfast place. My excitement was indescribable.

I mentioned to Jack that my English girlfriend and her family were coming from Yorkshire to pay me a visit. He thought it was a wonderful idea and suggested that I tell the camp commander, but not to mention that she was my girl friend. The commander would have to give written consent for me to leave the camp and spend the day with the family because they would most likely take me more than five miles from the camp. Mr. Ridgway would also have to sign a note every time he picked me up, to say that he took full responsibility for me while I was with them. Jack didn't think that there would be a problem as long I took care of the mail.

I hardly closed my eyes all night, wondering what it would be like to see Sue again, wondering if she had changed a little, wondering if the family would be allowed inside the camp. I would be proud to show them my post office and the place where I lived.

The following day, although I had a hard time concentrating on my work, I managed to get an appointment with the new commander. I found he was a very nice person. He assured me that it would be all right for the Ridgways to come and visit me, as long as I took care of my postal duties. They could pick me up in the morning and bring me back at night. I was thrilled to think that I would be allowed to spend a whole day with them while they were here.

Tel: Sawtry 55 & 18

P.O. W. PASS

No.:-.. A 878368 .... Rank:-.... Ogefr. ....Name:-.. Kern, K

of 59 POW Camp, Wood Walton Lane, Sawtry-Hunts

has authority to proceed beyond the 5 mile limit of this Camp for the purpose of Visiting/Proceeding to...Peterborough

between the hours.... 10.00 .... to.. 22.00 ....hrs, on 26. 3. 48

Issued at
Sawtry Camp   (R.T. Hook)   Capt.
                               Adjutant, No. 59 German POW Camp.

Date:-.. 26. 3. 48

Here is the original permit issued by the Commander.

My work in the post office was very demanding. All the men in the camp were allowed to receive personal mail. Only once in a while was I asked to hold the mail for the commander to look through it, and very seldom did he open a letter and read it. Whenever he did, I had to reseal it and the commander put a label on it, to say it had been censored.

When I had some spare time during the day I went for a walk with Struppie. Once in a while, when he was not on a leash, he would chase a rat and instantly kill it. He never lost one. He was by now very obedient to me, except when it came to rats. Nothing in the world would stop him when he was chasing one.

While I was in the village, I looked in on the Pettifer family. Mrs. Pettifer, as always very polite and friendly, asked me to come into the house. She was very excited to hear about the upcoming performance that our group in the camp was putting on for anyone who wanted to attend. We had quite a nice size band and also an amateur acting group, which put on plays. They usually performed outdoors, unless the weather was bad, in which case it was held in a large military tent, and the number of spectators had to be restricted. There was a small fee to get in, the proceeds of which were used to buy new instruments for the band.

During our conversation I told Mrs. Pettifer about Sue's family coming to visit and asked if she knew of a bed and breakfast place near by. She recommended a nice little place approximately three miles away and promised to have the address and phone number the next time I was in the area.

On our way back to the British compound, I stopped to pick a few buttercups to cheer up my room. Before we got to the gate I met with one of the tailors, who lived in a Nissen hut on the outskirts of the camp. These men made tailor-made uniforms for the officers of the camp staff.

We talked a little about home and family. His brother was a prisoner of war in Russia. His family was all right but they hadn't heard a word from his brother.

I told him that I was going to have visitors from Bradford, and wondered if he could make me a jacket and a pair of trousers, without the yellow sun and the yellow stripes on them. He promised that he would if I could do him a favor also. He wanted me to send a parcel for him without it being checked.

It was agreed that he would bring his parcel to my office and then measure me for a new outfit there. I was thrilled to think that I would have something nice to wear when Sue and her parents came to visit.

Every time I walked around outside the camp, I was reminded of the beautiful trees that grew in the part of Germany where I came from. We owned a large fruit orchard and I spent a lot of time there with my brother and sisters when we were children.

I wondered what kind of help my father would have to take care of all the trees and to cut the grass for our caged rabbits. When the apples and pears started to ripen, my brother and I would go to the orchard after school and at weekends. It was a good half hour's walk from our house. We gathered all the fallen fruit for my mother to make jelly. We also grew our own vegetables, and though we had to carry the water from a small brook nearby, we had a lot of fun doing it. I figured that my sisters would have to do all that kind of work now.

I took Struppie to the kitchen to pick up some food for him and to have some supper and a 'cuppa' [cup of tea] myself. Jack was there too and he told me that the camp commander had suggested that I act as assistant interpreter in emergencies. The other interpreter, whose name was Bruno, was frequently not available. Usually an interpreter was needed when one of our men was punished, or if there was an accident, or someone was taken to hospital.

I reminded Jack that when I had parcels to get ready for the post office, I practically worked all day and all night. He assured me that they had thought about getting me some extra help for a day or two, when I was overloaded with work.

The next morning, there was a letter from Sue. I couldn't wait until I had delivered the rest of the mail so I opened it right there in the guardhouse. She informed me that they would be coming to visit me on Saturday, July 17th, only six days away. I started to count the days, hours and minutes until we were together again.

I looked in on the tailor, to see how he was progressing with my tailor-made uniform. The jacket was ready and I thought it looked beautiful. It was shorter than the standard British army jacket, with a zipper in the front instead of buttons. It looked better on me than the long one, which I was issued with, because I am not very tall. The tailor told me that the trousers would be ready in about two days and added in a whisper that he would bring them to the post office with another parcel for Germany. I assured him that was all right.

The next lot of 90 parcels was ready for inspection. Though a lot of the original restrictions had been eased, each parcel still had to be presented in an open condition, so that all the contents could be checked by the captain. That could take hours, depending on what kind of mood the captain was in and how busy his schedule was.

Jack and I then took them to my post office and I had to wrap them all, checking each address and making sure everything was correct before I could take them to the village post office.

That evening, a young man called Fritz was sent to my post office by the German camp commander to help me out. I showed him how to rewrap parcels and to get them ready. I noticed that he had very nice handwriting and all his work was very neat.

In the early morning hours we were finally finished and we had a cup of coffee and a chat. He said that he would be helping me for another two days and that he did all of the office work for our German camp commander.

The next morning Jack, Fritz and I drove into the village to mail our cargo of 93 parcels. As usual, we had a good chat with Ken, who was always very friendly and had a joke or two to tell us. Ken said to me, "If you keep this up I am going to have to hire extra help." I told him that I already had help, and introduced Fritz to him.

On our way back we stopped off at Jack's girlfriend's house. He suggested we go for a walk until he returned. That was perfectly all right with us as we usually had some time to spare after we had delivered parcels.

It was a beautiful day, sunny with just a few clouds in the sky. We followed a small stream until we came to some willows where the grass was lush and green. We sat down and talked.

Fritz came from the northeast of Germany. He was very tall with wavy blond hair and clear blue eyes, typical of that region. He told me his family was OK but the Russians occupied the area and that when his repatriation came around, he would not go back to where his parents lived. He had served his apprenticeship as an accountant and he didn't trust the Russians. By the way his parents worded their letter, he could tell that they were afraid it would be censored, and they were not telling him what was actually going on. He had a friend in Bavaria, which was occupied by Americans, and he would give that as his home address.

After a while, Fritz fell asleep, lying in the grass. I lay beside him, resting my head on my hands and gazing up at the sky. It felt good to feel the warmth of the sun on my face. Watching the clouds go by gave me such a feeling of peace and tranquility, and I let my thoughts wander.

I saw my life drifting by before me. I felt that three years of war and over two years as a prisoner were a long time out of my young life to be wasted. I vividly remembered the time we were being heavily shelled by the enemy. Our unit was seeking shelter at a farmyard in Belgium. While some of us were in the cellar below, we had some direct hits on the farmhouse above us. The results were devastating.

I was hit by shrapnel, but thanks to my leather map case, my injuries were very slight. The leather case took the brunt of the blast. My friend next to me however, who was also my machine gunner, lost both of his legs. One of them was completely ripped off and the other one was only dangling on bits of flesh. I carried him across my shoulders to the nearest field hospital, which was only about 200 feet away.

On the way there we were barraged by grenade fire. My friend, who amazingly was conscious in spite of his severe injuries, begged me to leave him and seek shelter for myself. To my deep sorrow, when I finally got him there, he had slipped out of this world. [He had just returned from leave, during which he got married.]

My thoughts came back to where I was, lying in the grass, alive and well. I realized that I should thank God for having spared me such terrible suffering, instead of complaining.

The sound of the Land Rover's horn brought me back to reality. Jack had ended his visit with his girlfriend and we returned to camp.

Before it got dark I took Struppie for a walk through the fields. Some of the farmers were making hay. It reminded me of the days when as boys we used to help the farmers in our village bring in the hay. I noticed dragonflies dancing and hovering over a pond. Their wings were shimmering in the evening sun and reflecting all the colors of the rainbow.

Struppie watched them, as fascinated as I was. I was very glad that Struppie had found the door to my Nissen hut, and that I had him as a friend. Sometimes I even talked to him in German and he seemed to understand me.

On Friday I arranged for a meeting with the colonel, the camp commander, to make certain that the arrangements were all right for the visit of Sue's parents. He told me that he would leave a paper at the guardhouse, which her father had to sign each morning when they came to pick me up. I also had to be signed back in, in the evening. He assured me that I could bring them into the camp to show them my post office and the place where I lived.

The evening went by very quickly. My smart new outfit was ready and I had also acquired a tie and a new blue air force shirt from the quartermaster, for whom I did a favor once in a while. I cleaned my place up and tried to make it look nice. Besides the clothes I wore, I didn't have many possessions.

My bed consisted of a wooden frame with a straw mattress, very plain but luxurious compared to the rest of the men in the camp. There was also a small table and a chair. Chairs were unheard of in the barracks. At the foot of the bed I had a blanket laid on the floor, which was Struppie's bed and no doubt a luxury for a farm dog. Besides that, I had a wall shelf, which was given to me by my friend Jack. On it I had an ashtray and a coffee mug, given me by the canteen. At the very end of the shelf stood my most precious possession, a picture of my darling Sue. A luxurious 'apartment' for a prisoner of war.

There was one more thing I still had to do, and that was to give Struppie a wash. I wanted him to look his best for Saturday. Most wash places in the camp were nothing but a metal roof over a row of taps.

The shower was next to it and consisted of four posts with a corrugated iron roof. The sides were about three feet of corrugated iron, which started about 18 inches up from the ground. Otherwise it was open. One did not see many men using the shower on a cold day, because there was no hot water.

This evening I got a bucket of hot water from the kitchen and gave Struppie a good wash in front of my Nissen hut. He didn't care much for water and snarled at me. Since it was a warm evening I let him run, so that he could shake himself dry.

Now all the preparations were taken care of and I just hoped that the weather would cooperate for the weekend.

I realized that this would be the first time we had a chance to be together without having to worry about being seen or caught. We had had two years of hiding and dodging guards, always having to look over our shoulders for fear of being seen. It was an unusual way to fall in love. But as Sue once wrote in one of her letters, no one would ever be able to stop us from loving each other. I wouldn't have missed one minute of it. Being in love was a beautiful thing, especially as a prisoner of war.

28

It was a beautiful day when I woke up. I got up early, because I wanted to make sure that all my work was taken care of by noon. The Ridgway family was on their way, and would be arriving around 2:00 p.m.

When I picked up the mail I found to my surprise that Sue had sent me a parcel with all sorts of goodies, including some cigarettes. There was also a letter in which she told me that both her mother and father were very much looking forward to meeting me, and that she couldn't wait for the moment when we were in each other's arms.

My mind was not on my work that morning, but finally at around 11:30, I had finished all my deliveries. I went back to feed Struppie and get myself ready.

This time I didn't have to make sure that Heinz and Seppie were watching out for guards, nor did I have to crawl through barbed wire. It was hard for me to believe that this time it was OK for me, a prisoner of war, to meet my sweetheart's family.

I went to the guardhouse to make certain the papers were in order. Then I walked about 50 yards along the road, in the direction that I hoped they would be coming from. Sitting down near the roadside I watched every car that came by. I had no idea what their car looked like.

A good hour must have gone by when I decided to get up and stand for a while. Suddenly I heard the screech of tires and saw a red car pulling up by the side of the road ahead of me. Then Sue was getting out and running towards me and we were in each other's arms. I could have kissed and held her forever, until she said, "Oh Karl, I am so glad I am here, come and meet my family."

When I left my Nissen hut in the morning I thought that I was prepared for this, but I realized I wasn't. Sue must have sensed the way I felt. She took me by the arm saying, "Come on Karl. I think they will like you," and we both walked over to the car.

Her mother was the first one to get out of the car. She looked very kind and loving. She had very fine features and was quite a lot taller than Sue. With an honest smile on her face, she held out her hand to shake mine, and then gave me a hug.

Next came Sue's father. He was tall and very handsome with a firm and genuine handshake. He said laughing, "I really had to brake hard when Sue called out that we had just driven past you."

Then the girls got out of the car. The older one, Pat, was tall and slender and reminded me of a ballerina. The last one to greet me was the little one. She said shyly, "Hello, I am Daisy."

Now that the introductions were over I felt much better. We all got into the car. I sat in the back seat between Pat and Sue and Daisy sat on my lap. We drove to the guardhouse to take care of the formalities and then I suggested they have a look at my post office and the place where I lived.

As we arrived in front of my Nissen hut, Struppie started barking excitedly. I called out to him that I was with friends. Once we were inside he went from one to the other, making their acquaintance.

We were just about to go over and look at the post office when Sue noticed that someone had left a cake on my shelf. The note next to it read *Welcome, from all your friends at the camp!* I had an idea it was our German camp commander who had it baked for us. Before I could offer everyone a piece of cake I realized that I had nothing to offer to drink with it.

I decided to go to the kitchen with Sue to find out if someone could make us some tea. The kitchen was just across the street from where I lived. We left everyone behind with Struppie and went to ask one of the cooks for a jug of tea, some cups, and a knife to cut the cake.

It felt like a party, all of us sitting on my bed enjoying the dessert, which was like a delicious German gateau. Everyone loved it.

We called in at my post office next door and then went for a ride through Connington. We stopped by the Pettifer's house and had a nice visit with them. Sue's father was very interested when Mr. Pettifer told him about the art of roof thatching.

Towards evening Sue's parents asked me to come with them for supper at a place they had been recommended by the people they were staying with. We had a good meal and when we came out of the restaurant it was nearly time for me to be back at the camp.

We sat in the car and discussed what we would do the next day. Sue's father thought it would be nice to go for a picnic, and everyone agreed. I told them about the meadows and the brook, where I waited for the lance corporal, and it was decided that we would go there.

Mr. Ridgway signed me back in at the guardhouse and we drove to my Nissen hut. It was a perfect summer evening and I asked the family if they would mind waiting at my place while Sue and I took Struppie for a walk. Daisy asked if she could come too, but her mother said quickly, "No Daisy, you stay here with us."

Finally we were alone together. We sat on a bench behind the Nissen hut and held each other tight. We sat in silence under a starry sky. We let our hearts do the talking.

Sue broke the silence by whispering, "Oh Karl, I love you with all my heart. Why do we always have to leave each other? Please tell me it won't be long before we can be together for ever."

"Oh Darling," I said, "so far our love has sustained us. Please promise me that you will wait for me." She confirmed it with a kiss.

Struppie was lying contentedly underneath the bench. As if Sue was reading my thoughts she asked, "What are you going to do with Struppie when you go back to Germany?" I told her that I hoped to find him a good home with one of the farmers, even though I would really love to stay and... Sue wouldn't let me finish the sentence. She agreed with her mother that I should go back to my family, as much as it was going to hurt both of us, it was the best thing to do. I kissed her and assured her that I would come back as soon as I possibly could.

Sue started crying softly at the thought of having to part. I held her against me and kissed her tenderly. Soon we had to go back in again. Sue brought out her handkerchief to wipe the lipstick off my face and then renewed her own lips.

Struppie ran ahead and scratched at the door and the family let him in. They were waiting for us. Sue's father said they had better leave right away before it got too late and they found themselves sleeping at my place. It was arranged that they would pick me up at the gate at 10 o'clock in the morning. All three girls in the back seat waved to me as they drove away.

Before I went to sleep I thought what a lovely family they were, not a bit false, and very nice to know. Not many parents would drive almost 300 miles out of their way so that their daughter could meet with her friend who was, of all things, a prisoner of war and a former enemy. More than anything, I liked the way they treated me with respect.

29

I had a very restful night. I hoped it was going to be a nice day, because I had no idea where to go if the weather changed and the picnic had to be canceled.

Promptly at 10 o'clock the Vauxhall pulled up in front of my place and Sue got out, looking beautiful in a sporty outfit. Everyone greeted me with a warm good morning.

Sue's mother asked if we could first look for a kettle. I understood that they wanted to see cattle and assured her that I knew where to go. So off we drove. I remembered where I had seen cows grazing in a field and led them there, while Sue's mother was wondering why I was taking them out into the fields to buy a kettle, and I was wondering why they wanted to see cattle if they lived in the country.

Before long I pointed to some cows grazing in a field and the misunderstanding came to light. Sue's father stopped the car so he could laugh his heart out. We all ended up doing the same while her mother explained that she needed a kettle to boil water. I felt a bit of a fool and apologized.

We drove into Connington and found a shop that sold exactly what Sue's mother was looking for. They had brought a camping stove with them, but forgotten to bring the kettle to boil water for tea.

It turned out to be a beautiful hot day. The sun was out and the clouds we had seen earlier in the morning had disappeared. We set off for the nice quiet spot near the small brook. As we were driving along, Sue burst out laughing every so often at the thought of me, leading them into the fields to buy a kettle. Her giggling set off both her sisters. After a while I said, "OK girls, one day you may learn German, and then it will be me who is doing the giggling."

It was a perfect place for a picnic. The air was filled with the smell of fresh hay, which the farmer had not taken into the barn yet.

We all helped with the unloading. First came the blankets, which Sue's father and I spread out on the ground to sit on. Mother and the girls unloaded the picnic basket, drinks and food while he got the little stove going to boil the water for tea. They had brought two bottles of water with them from the place where they stayed.

Sue and her mother made sandwiches for us all. There was quite a variety including corned beef, cheddar cheese, and Bovril. For dessert we had scones and biscuits. I had a wonderful time and felt so grateful to Sue's parents for the way they made me feel like one of them.

After eating we sat and talked for a long time. This was the first opportunity Sue's parents had to find out more about me and my family. They wanted to know about my profession and what I intended to do after my repatriation. They were very interested in the things I told them about my homeland and about how I came to be taken prisoner.

After some time Daisy became bored and wanted to play. I got the idea of building a make-believe horse and carriage. I made the carriage out of hay and asked the little one to sit in it. Then I went in front of it and pretended to be the horse. We both had a great time.

Afterwards I showed them some of the acrobatics I used to do when I was in my late teens. I did cartwheels, handstands, headstands, and what we called flick-flacks, when you leap backwards in the air onto your hands, and then back again onto your feet, several times.

In the early afternoon Sue's mother and the two girls were gathering flowers. Her father was taking a little nap on the blanket. Now was our chance to sneak off for a while. I pressed Sue's hand a little tighter and said, "Would you like to go for a walk?" She nodded quickly and got up to go.

By now the sun was very hot. I had taken my jacket off and rolled up my shirtsleeves. Sue was in a light sundress, which made her look more beautiful then ever. She called out to her mother to let her know that we were taking a walk. Arm in arm we walked towards some haystacks. Sue said, "This must be one of the most beautiful days of my life."

We sat down on the hay and kissed, and kissed, and kissed.

Time stood still for us, until we heard Daisy call out, "Sue, where are you? We are all getting hungry and Daddy wants to leave soon."

Sue answered, "Here we are Daisy."

I watched to see which side of the haystack she was coming from, then just as she was asking where I was, I sneaked up behind her and lifted her up in the air and said, "Here I am little Daisy."

She laughed and said, "Let's play airplane." I asked her to hold firmly onto my hand. With my other hand I held her ankle and whirled her round like an airplane, until we were both out of breath. Now Pat came looking for us.

When we got back, Sue's mother remarked what a beautiful day it had been. I said it went by far too fast for me. Everyone helped to load the picnic basket, stove, and blankets into the trunk of the car. Sue's mother must have sensed my sadness because she said, "I know Karl, that you would like us to stay longer, but it will take us a whole day to get to Bridlington, where we had planned to spend our vacation."

We drove towards Peterborough and found a pub, which served fish and chips, something I had never eaten before. The girls tried to convince me that it was very good.

We got a table to ourselves in a corner. Sue's father said he was going to have a beer and asked if I wanted one. I told him that I hadn't had a beer for so long I had probably forgotten what it tastes like. When the beer came, Sue's mother whispered to me, "Just drink it slowly Karl". Since I hadn't had any alcohol for such a long time, I thought that was good advice.

Mother ordered fish and chips for everyone and hot tea for the rest of the family. We had very little fish back home in Germany and I was surprised how delicious it tasted. I was very hungry too. After we were all finished eating, Sue's father suggested we drive back to the camp and go for a walk together while it was still daylight. I thought that was a splendid idea and mentioned that we could take Struppie with us.

Back at the Nissen hut, Struppie was waiting for us. I let him out and then fed him before we all set out on our walk. Daisy took Struppie's lead. She told me that they had a black labrador at home called Sally, who was being looked after by their neighbor.

Our walk was enjoyable. Daisy ran ahead, having fun with Struppie. I walked with Sue's parents so that we could talk. Sue's mother promised to send parcels to my family if I told her what they needed most.

When we came to the small pond, the girls and Struppie were fascinated by the dragonflies. Since it was Sunday evening there was no one else around. We sat down on the grass and watched the midges and dragonflies dancing in the warm evening sun. Sue sat next to me and squeezed my hand every so often. I leaned over and gave her a kiss on the cheeks.

In the distance a farmer was making hay. I just loved the smell of hay mixed with all the fragrances of flowers around us. There were buttercups and daisies growing around the edge of the pond. Behind us was a hedge of blooming wild roses mixed with white hawthorn. At the edge of the path I noticed some larkspur and, just barely above the ground, some milkweed that looked like a white blanket. Everything was growing in profusion. I asked Pat and Daisy to pick some wild flowers for me to put in a glass jar and remind me of their visit. They soon came back with a handful of flowers.

The sun was much lower by now and we could feel an evening breeze blowing. As everyone was getting up to walk back to my place, Sue's grip tightened around my arm. We waited till the family had walked ahead some distance and then, under the cover of the wildrose hedge, we embraced and kissed each other passionately. I put my hands around her face, looked into her beautiful eyes, and said, "I know, Darling, that the day will come when we will not have to part any more. I promise that I will remain true to you until that day."

Tears were rolling down her face as she said, "I love you so much Karl and there will never be any one else besides you."

I kissed the tears from her face and assured her that our love would see us through. Daisy came running along the path towards us with

Struppie pulling her behind him, and we rejoined the others. As usual, Sue made sure that I had no lipstick showing on my face before we got there.

It was time to say goodbye. Sue's mother said it had been wonderful meeting me and that I had a lot to look forward to, meeting my family after so many years. She gave me a hug and said, "Don't worry my dear, time will sort everything out."

Mr. Ridgway wished me all the best and hoped we would meet again. He added, "It was a pleasure meeting you Karl." Pat and Daisy also gave me a hug and they all got in the car.

My heart was heavy as I turned to Sue. She was choking back the tears as she told me that she would wait for me. Then she took out her handkerchief to wave to me until they were out of sight.

30

The next morning I rose early. While I was getting shaved and dressed I thought about the Ridgway family on their way to the seaside.

When I picked the mail up I found a letter from my family. They had received a lovely parcel from the Ridgways. They were thrilled about the sugar, the flour and also the chocolate, and asked me to write and thank them on their behalf.

They also mentioned that my brother Walter, who was a fighter pilot flying over Russia, was officially reported missing in action. In a letter from his commander they had been informed that although they searched the area where he was believed shot down, they had found no trace of the airplane. It happened about four weeks before the war ended.

I had always been very close to my brother. He was two years older than I and also taller and stronger. I had great respect for him. I felt very sad to think that I would probably never see him again.

During the afternoon the German camp commander paid me a visit. He told me that during the next two months about 80 men would be repatriated from our camp, but my name was not on the list.

For the next few days I was kept very busy with my postal duties. I received a letter and a postcard from Sue, mailed from Bridlington. Her parents, she said, seemed to like me very much. They admitted to her that they were very skeptical before they met me, especially her father, but felt much better about it, now that they had got to know me a little. Sue said that she missed me terribly and she would much rather be with me, no matter where it was, than on holiday. I missed them all too. I felt that I had found a new family.

In another letter Sue wrote me that she had met my dear friend Heinz and that he now had a girlfriend who lived close by. My other friend, Seppie, had been moved to another camp. She didn't know where. She also sent me cigarettes, chocolates, writing paper and a few pieces of clear plastic. I had started another bracelet for her but couldn't finish it because I didn't have enough material. Her father had asked if I could make him a cigarette holder like the one I had made for myself, out of toothbrush handles and in different colors.

My work at the post office had almost doubled. There were no restrictions on how many letters could be sent. One parcel per month was allowed. However, each parcel still had to be censored by the captain in charge. I had to be there as the interpreter and afterwards pack and wrap them all. Many a night I worked till early morning to get the mail to the village post office.

Sue and I wrote to each other at least twice a week and worried if we didn't hear anything within three days. She kept me well informed about the camp in Yorkshire. Heinz had been moved away to another camp and Seppie was getting ready to be repatriated back to Germany.

Communications with Germany were now open and we got to know what was happening at home. Unfortunately there was a lot of sad news. There was hardly enough food to go around. In many ways we were better off here in the prison camps. At least we didn't have to beg for food.

The summer was almost over and there was a whiff of fall in the air. One morning there was especially dense fog. Shortly after the trucks had left to take the men to work, we received word of an accident. One of the trucks carrying about 30 men had collided in dense fog with another vehicle at an intersection about 15 miles from the camp. Most of the men were injured, some severely and some had even been killed.

News reached us that the ambulance, on its way from the city, had collided with a bus. A doctor and an interpreter were badly needed to help with the injured and to translate for the medics. We were all frantically trying to find the doctor and the interpreter. After some time the doctor and his assistant were located, but no one knew where the interpreter was.

A Land Rover was ready to leave as soon as everyone was there. By now the fog was so thick that one could hardly see the side of the road. The captain told me that he wanted me to go along to interpret for them, as he didn't want to delay leaving any longer. I joined the doctor and his assistant at the back of the open vehicle. The captain got in next to the driver and we headed towards the gate.

We were just turning the corner onto the road when the interpreter finally turned up and he quickly changed places with me. I watched the car disappear down the road.

About an hour after they left, a car driven by a civilian pulled up in front of my Nissen hut. He brought news that the Land Rover had had a head-on collision with another vehicle just before they got to the scene of the accident. Everyone in the Land Rover was badly injured except for the driver. The doctor and the interpreter were both in hospital with broken backs.

It made shivers go down my spine, to think I could have been one of those in hospital with a broken back. A few days later the commander took me with him to visit all the injured at the hospital. Their condition was very serious. Somehow the good Lord must have looked out for me.

When I was repatriated about eight months later, the interpreter was still in hospital and so was the doctor. Both were paralyzed from the neck down. I never found out what eventually happened to them.

October and November were very hectic. I was called upon several times to interpret in injury cases. Once, one of our men was stung on the tongue by a wasp. His tongue swelled up so much that he had to be rushed to hospital. He did not speak any English so I had to go along as interpreter. He was given some medication, which brought down the swelling, and he was released the next day.

Repatriations were going on every week. One morning I read an article in the newspaper, which said that any of us who received an invitation from a family could get permission to stay with that family over the Christmas holidays. The address had to be within a radius of 100 miles from the camp and the stay was limited to three days. I was excited at the possibility of being able to spend Christmas with Sue's family, even though I knew it was more than 100 miles away.

Jack came to tell me that he had become engaged over the weekend and that his fellow soldiers were giving him a party in the canteen. He invited me to join them. I told him I would look forward to it.

While I was eating supper in the kitchen, I asked the sergeant if he had a good map of England, so that I could find out the distance from Connington to Bradford. We worked out that it was approximately 150 miles. This made me feel rather disheartened, but I was determined to get around the distance problem, even if I had to see the camp commander personally.

A lot of our men were making toys and gifts for Christmas. I planned to make a doll's cradle for Daisy, a cigarette holder for Sue's father, a plastic heart for Pat, an inkstand for Sue, and a napkin holder for her mother. I planned to send them a parcel about two weeks before Christmas. However I still secretly hoped I could take it with me and give my presents to each one personally.

When Jack came in the morning he confirmed that what I had read in the paper was true, and that everyone who had an invitation was responsible for his own fare.

After we had finished our work at the post office, Jack took me to the train station to find out how much the fare was to Bradford. I was at least ten pounds short to pay for it. That didn't concern me too much because I could always ask Sue to lend me the money. But I was still 50 miles over the limit and that was more worrying.

Jack's engagement party went well. Apart from myself, our German camp leader and a driver were invited. The other driver and the interpreter were still seriously ill in hospital. The captain had a broken leg but was otherwise OK.

I asked Jack what he thought I should do to be able to visit Bradford at Christmas. He thought Sue's parents could send a letter to the camp commander, asking him to make an exception in my case. At the same time it would be a good idea for me to meet with him personally. I should tell him that I would work day and night, if need be, to make sure that the mail was taken care of right up to Christmas.

I wrote to Sue to let her know about the newspaper article. Maybe, if her parents wrote a convincing letter, the commander would soften and give me permission to go to Bradford.

I mailed the letter the next day. Two days later I received a letter from Sue, telling me about the newspaper article and full of hope that I could visit them.

Christmas was approaching fast. I had all my presents ready for the

Monday morning 1.12.47

My Dearest Vali,

    We have just got the order about spending Xmas with an Engl. Family. Now I should like to let you know it, because it is important. With my love the order says:

    All P.o.W.'s are allowed to be absent on Xmas for Dec. 24th 2 p.m. to Dec. 26th 6 p.m. under following conditions:

1.) An invitation must be sent to the Commandant of the prisoner concerned, in which is explained, that the host will take the full responsibility for the P.o.W.

2.) If the Commandant gives approval.

3.) The distance must not be more then 100 miles.

4.) The cost of the fare must be guaranteed, either by the host, or by the P.o.W.

                                            P.T.O.

So Vali dearest if your Father is writing, will you please ask him to consider "№ 1."

The address he must write to is:

             To the Commandant

               39 P.o.W. Camp

               Hood Hatton Lane,

                      Gate Sawtry, Hunts

Well I will have to close now and remain once again

             with lots of love

                 and thousands of Kisses

                     your Sweetheart

                          Karl

Ridgway family and a lot of work keeping up with all the parcels going to Germany. All repatriations were stopped until after the holidays.

Sue sent me another letter and enclosed ten pounds towards my fare to Bradford. Everything was set for the trip, except that I had not heard anything from the commander yet.

Jack arrived to take me to the Connington post office. He told me that he was going to speak to the commander on my behalf and he would tell him that he was willing to fill in for me should the need arise. He was not getting any leave over the holidays and was going to spend Christmas day with his fiancée. What a generous and kind person he was. I thanked him with all my heart.

When we were through at the post office, Jack steered towards his fiancée's house. Since the weather was cold, he asked me to come into the house with him. His fiancée received me with a very warm welcome and served us a nice cup of tea with some scones. She insisted I look at the photographs of their engagement. When I asked about their plans for the future, she said they were going to live in her parents' house until after we were all repatriated.

After nearly two hours Jack thought we had better get back to the camp. I had not been in my post office long, when Jack came in, followed by the camp commander.

The commander said that Jack had spoken to him about my visit to Sue's family in Yorkshire and also he had received the invitation from Mr. and Mrs. Ridgway. According to the rules, he would normally have to turn down my request. However, because of the excellent report he had received from the lance corporal, he was making an exception in my case.

I had to promise not to broadcast this around and that I would do whatever it took to take care of the mail before I left. I promised that I would and thanked him for being so kind to me and said, "Sir, you can't imagine what this means to me."

"But I do," he said. He would write to the Ridgway family to let them know I had permission to visit and I should be receiving a piece of paper to confirm it. I wished him a wonderful holiday and he wished me the same.

I could have hugged Jack for what he did for me. Instead I thanked him several times.

Extracts from a letter to Sue:

10 Dec. 1947
My own dearest Sweetheart Ursula,
    I am sitting in my office Darling writing this letter. This morning I mailed a letter to you, which I wrote in a hurry, late last night, to let you know our new camp number. Our new address is #59 POW Camp, Wood Walton Lane, Sawtry, Hunts. I hope you will have received that letter in the meantime. Well my love, at first I want to thank you so very much for the two letters which I received. Oh dearest I was so very pleased about them, Especially the one I received last night. Please forgive me for not being able to write sooner in answer to your previous letter. I have such a lot to do before the Christmas Holiday. On top of everything, they took away my helper. He was moved some where else. So all the work at the post office is left for me to do myself.
    You may hardly believe this, but I couldn't find time to do anything for myself during the last three weeks. There is one consolation; it'll be much easier again after Christmas. However my Darling, I don't care how much work I have. Knowing, that we will be together in two weeks, makes me feel very happy, because it seems like eternity since we were in each other's arms.
    Well dearest Sue, thank you so much making inquiries for me about trains leaving Peterborough on the 24th of Dec. I don't know yet, which one I will be able to take. Much depends on when I get through with all my mail. Hopefully, I will be able to leave early in the morning, since there is no mail delivery on Christmas Eve. I will let you know in good time, so that you can arrange to meet me in with your father. Please tell your father that I am very thankful for every thing he did for me, to make this visit possible.
    I am very pleased to be able to tell you, that the swelling I had on my eye is much better. It is not completely healed yet, but I am sure, everything will be fine by the time I see you. Yes Darling I know that I should keep my eyes warm and also give them rest. Unfortunately, neither warmth nor rest is easy to come by at the moment. With the weather being so cold, I don't get enough coke, nor wood, to keep my living quarters warm enough, which does not help my sore eyes either. I am

much better off however, than most of my fellow prisoners. They don't get enough wood to keep those large barracks warm. To keep from getting too cold, most of them lay down under their blankets, after they get home from work with their clothes on.

Even though my eyes are not quite healed dearest, once I will be able to look into your beautiful tender eyes, will make all the difference. I simply can't wait to hold you close to me. My heart longs to be with you. So you will see, being with you will be the best medicine anyone could prescribe for me. I am already starting to count the days, the hours, and later the minutes until we are close to each other again. My greatest wish for a Christmas present is to be near you. So close, that I will be able to feel your heart beat against mine. To feel your tender lips touch mine, is all I long for.

Now I have a question that has been on my mind. I am wondering how many guests do you expect to be at your house for Christmas? How many aunts and uncles and other relatives will join us? I am hoping my love, that there won't be too many because I think that will make me feel very shy. Hopefully we will have some time by ourselves. Don't you Darling?

Well my dearest, I received a letter from home, in which my sisters tell me that they received the letter, which you wrote and I translated for them a little while ago. They want me to say thank you for them. The parcel you sent however has not arrived. For to day I will say good night to you and remain as always,

yours forever

Karl

PS: many greetings to your parents and sisters, also Lorna and Kathy. I shall be so happy to see you very soon.

I was indeed counting the days. My biggest concern was that my eyes would heal completely and that I would feel well. I had an appointment with the camp doctor twice a week. His treatment seemed to be working, and he thought that I should be all right.

Jack came to take me to the train station to purchase my ticket. He greeted me with his usual cheerful good morning, and invited me to the sergeant's mess for breakfast. He mentioned that the colonel had already left for his Christmas vacation and the captain was standing in for him. He himself was taking his leave over the New Year holidays.

Both the colonel and the captain were very fair men, which made camp life much more bearable. I heard that quite a number of our men got permission to visit with various English families.

I wondered if my family would have a real Christmas tree, like we used to when we were children. When Christmas approached, we used to watch our mother baking all sorts of goodies. She had to hide them from us otherwise there wouldn't have been many left by the time Christmas Eve came around.

I can remember my brother and I going with our father into the woods, to a designated area, to pick out a tree, cut it, and then carry it home. That was quite a treat for us. I doubted if they would be able to do that. From what I had heard, they wouldn't be able to have much of anything. Sue's mother had sent them a parcel of food and I was able to send some flour and sugar. So hopefully they would be able to bake a few cookies.

Sue wrote me that with all the excitement and anticipation of my visit, she didn't sleep any more at night. She couldn't wait until she was in my arms. She mentioned that there would be a lot of her relatives at their house on Christmas Eve. She did not say that they were anxious to meet me, which left me somewhat apprehensive. Being behind barbed wire for three years, isolated from the general public, didn't exactly boost my confidence. I hoped that I wouldn't have to socialize too much.

Before going to bed that night I paid a visit next door where the two drivers lived, and told them that I needed to be taken to Peterborough early morning on Christmas Eve. They assured me that one of them would be able to take me there. (I had done them favors in the past too). Kurt came with me to the canteen for breakfast, a nice hot cup of tea with bacon and scrambled egg.

After our short trip to the Connington post office, I asked Jack to come into my hut with me if he had a few minutes to spare. I had a little present for him as a thank you for all he had done for me. It was a pen holder, similar to the one I made for Sue. In the front I had engraved his name, and at the bottom I wrote *Christmas 1947 from your friend Karl.* He was very pleased and said that he would treasure it and always remember me as his German friend.

Sue had once told me that one of her uncles was very much against her being friendly with a German prisoner of war. I started to worry if he was going to be there on Christmas Eve. If he were, I would just have to show him that I was a normal human being like everyone else.

The last day before my trip to Bradford was finally here. All my parcels were wrapped with the names on. Apart from that, all I had were the clothes I stood up in, so I was going to travel light.

Before the day was out, Jack came to look in on me to let me know that I needn't worry about the mail. For one thing, he didn't think there would be much, and whatever there was, he would take care of it.

My friend the tailor had made a good size bag for me to carry all my gifts in. It was made from a piece of canvas, lined with silk. It even had leather straps and a pocket on one side. I was very proud of it. To be sure that I didn't forget, I put my train tickets into the pocket of the bag before I went to bed.

I also took Struppie for a walk. He must have sensed that I was going somewhere without him because he never left my side the whole evening. Since we had no parcels in the post office, I let him sleep at the foot of my bed.

Bradford, England

31

It was still very dark when I woke up. I was dressed and ready long before 7:00 a.m., which was the time we had to leave. I went across to the canteen for some breakfast and met the driver there. One of the kitchen staff offered to make me a sandwich to take with me on the journey and I accepted gratefully. I thought how lucky I was to be treated so nicely.

Promptly at 7:00 the driver pulled up outside my Nissen hut. For the first time in three years I was going to travel on my own, with no guards to accompany me, and I didn't have to worry about being seen. It would take a little while to get used to this freedom.

The driver told me to phone the guardhouse after I got back and someone would pick me up at the railway station. He dropped me off and there I was, all by myself.

I had about half an hour until my train left. I entered a large hall and found the notice board, which directed me to the platform from which the train left for Leeds. In Leeds I had to change trains.

The carriage in which I traveled was not very full so I could pick my seat. I sat near a window so that I could enjoy the scenery.

Not long after we left, the conductor came to check my ticket. He looked at me several times, as if he wasn't quite sure what to make of me. Before he could ask any questions, I showed him the letter from my camp commander. He seemed to be satisfied with that and wished me a nice trip.

From Leeds it was a short trip to my final destination. Before long the first houses of Bradford came in sight. Not long after that, I noticed the train was slowing down and heard the brakes being applied. As we rolled slowly into the station, the conductor called out, "Bradford, Bradford."

Everyone got up from their seats and made their way towards the nearest door. Though I had been waiting for so long to be with my sweetheart, I remained in my seat. I was in no great hurry and waited until everyone had left. Looking out of the window I didn't see Sue or her father and wondered what I would do if they were not there. I had brought their phone number with me but I had never used a telephone kiosk.

Finally I picked up my bag of presents and got off. People were still going back and forth along the platform. Sue spotted me first and came running towards me. With open arms she fell into mine. She said, "Oh Karl, we arrived a little late and I was afraid we might miss you, but now you are here, everything is all right."

I held her face in my hands and said, "You are as beautiful as ever and I love you."

She embraced me. "I love you too my darling."

We didn't have far to walk. When we got to the car, Sue motioned me to sit with her in the back. She had a lot to tell me about Heinz, Seppie and Theo, and about her new job.

When we pulled up in front of Highfield House, Clayton, Sue pointed towards some newly built homes. "See, this is where you used to work. It's the place where we first met." Most of the homes had been completed at the building site and the place looked so different that I didn't recognize it any more.

Sue must have noticed my nervousness. She kissed me tenderly. "There is no one in the house but my mother, Pat and Daisy, the rest of the family are not going to be here until this evening." She took my hand. "Come and meet them, they are anxious to see you again."

Daisy stretched out both of her hands towards me and said, "Welcome to my house." She seemed to have grown some since I saw her in the summer. Nevertheless, I picked her up high into the air and when I had put her back down she said, "I like you, are you going to stay with us for a while?" I told her yes, for three days. Sue's mother gave me a hug and offered me a cup of tea and some scones.

She asked me to make myself comfortable in the living room and Sue followed her mother into the kitchen to help her. Pat came to greet

House of Sue's parents at No. 14, Nab End, Clayton, Bradford, Yorkshire

me next. We shook hands, and she curtsied and said, "Nice to have you with us." She sat down next to me and pointed to a picture of herself in a ballet dress and ballet shoes, hanging on the wall. She told me that she was taking ballet lessons. Little Daisy quickly sat next to me also, announcing that she took ballet lessons too and went to fetch a picture of herself in a ballet dress.

Sue's father joined us and tea was served. They made me feel like one of the family.

I had a hand-drawn birthday card and a present for Sue, and a bar of chocolate each for Pat and Daisy. Sue's present was a bracelet I had made from small silver coins (threepenny bits). They were no longer in circulation and were hard to come by. Most of them had been sent to me by Sue's father. To make them into a bracelet, I had drilled two tiny holes on each side of the coin and connected them with a very thin silver wire. Jack had bought the clasp for me to complete it.

Sue was thrilled with her gift and the birthday card, which I had made out of a thin piece of cardboard. I had drawn flowers around the birthday greetings. Everyone thought it was beautifully done. Sue gave me a kiss, for the first time in front of the whole family. I couldn't miss the smile, which Pat and Daisy shared, when they saw their sister kissing me.

Sue's mother asked me to help them putting up the Christmas tree. Her father had bought it the day before, a beautiful big tree, and it was standing behind the house. It required two people to bring it in and put it in the stand.

We placed it next to the piano in the living room. I climbed the stepladder to reach the upper branches, and Pat and Daisy handed me the ornaments, with precise instructions where to hang them. Then they added strands of silver tinsel.

Mother was busy cooking a meal for us and Father gave me a glass of sherry with the words, "To a wonderful future to you, Karl." We sat down and talked. I told him about my Christmases as a young boy, and soon Sue's sisters came and sat on the floor in front of me, listening intently.

I explained how the five of us children had to stay in the kitchen while our parents put up the tree and decorated it. We were not allowed to see it being decorated. It always snowed on Christmas Eve, so we looked impatiently out of the window, watching the flakes come down and settling everywhere.

Often we saw people dressed as angels, going from house to house, carrying lanterns and singing Christmas carols. Every now and then we would open the kitchen door and call out, "Can't we come in yet?" However they made us wait till everything was ready. Finally we were invited into the living room, where we beheld a very festive sight. The candles on the tree were lit (they were regular candles, not electric lights) and we all sat around the tree, singing Christmas carols.

If we didn't see any gifts lying under the tree, we knew that Santa Claus was going to come in person. Our patience was tried again while we waited for him to knock at our door.

He arrived dressed in a long overcoat with a pointed cap and large boots. His long beard reached all the way down to his belt. On his back he carried a big sack with presents in it. In his other hand he carried a long broom or stick, which he threatened to use on anyone who had been naughty. Then he asked each of us if we had been good. If we said yes, and our parents confirmed it, he put down his sack and handed out the presents. As he was leaving we all thanked him and wished him a merry

Christmas. Now we could open the gifts and said thank you to our parents for giving them to Santa Claus.

Sue called us into the dining room for supper and Daisy told her, "Father Christmas doesn't come down the chimney in Germany, they actually see him when he comes to the house."

After supper mother told the girls to help clear the table before the visitors arrived. "They will be here very soon," she added.

Sue took me by the hand and said, "Come Karl, I will show you the rest of the house." All the rooms were very large with ten-foot high ceilings.

We went in the dining room first. The centerpiece was a beautiful table with eight high-backed chairs. In the corner stood a magnificent Chippendale sideboard. There was a chandelier and a very large picture window.

In the sitting room was a grand piano. There were four armchairs, each with a side table. On the walls hung beautiful pictures, a picture each of the two girls in their ballet dresses and a photo of Sue standing in the garden holding three little puppies. As we went through the long hallway I noticed a gorgeous looking antique grandfather clock. All the skirting boards and ceiling coves were of stained and polished hardwood.

The first room Sue showed me upstairs was her bedroom. As we got inside she quickly put her arms around me. I held her so close that we could feel each other's heartbeat. She whispered, "Oh Karl, I love you so much and I am so glad that you are here. I already dread the moment when you have to leave again, I miss you so very much when you are not near." We kissed passionately. She admitted that she fell in love with me the very first moment our eyes met at the little bridge I had built on the building site.

We were suddenly interrupted by Daisy, coming up the stairs and calling, "Mummy wants you to come down because the visitors will be here any moment." Sue wiped the lipstick from my face with her handkerchief, just before Daisy made it to the top of the stairs, and the three of us went down to join the rest of the family.

It wasn't long before the first visitors arrived. They were Sue's Uncle Cecil, Aunt Mabel, and her cousins Lorna and little Kathy. Then came Aunt Phyllis, mother's sister, and Uncle Harold her husband, with their sons Christopher and John. A little later Louis arrived, Uncle Cecil's eldest son. He had picked up Grandma Cooper, who lived in Bradford. We had a lovely evening. Uncle Cecil told me that he was a prisoner of war for a short while in Germany. So we had something in common.

Most of the evening I stayed close to Sue. I didn't want to be questioned too much by her curious relatives but I joined in everything they did. We had a glass of port wine and did a kind of dance where everybody joined in singing. It went like this, "You put your left foot in, your left foot out, you do the hokey-cokey and you turn about, that's what it's all about!" I joined in as best I could. I even did some acrobatic stunts, which I had learned as a youngster. All the relatives were very friendly towards me, especially Grandma Cooper, who I found a delightful person to be with. She was very genuine and understanding and I enjoyed her company from the moment we met. Aunt Mabel and Aunt Phyllis were the life and soul of the party.

I felt very much at home with everyone present. What I really enjoyed was singing Christmas carols, and when I didn't know the words in English, which was most of the time, I sang along in German. I even sang one carol all by myself in German, accompanied by little Daisy on the piano. We got quite a lot of applause.

Grandma Cooper stayed the night. Pat shared the bedroom with Sue. Daisy got to sleep with Grandma. Sue's father and I were to sleep in the living room. They had four very large armchairs. We put two together, facing each other, to make a very comfortable bed for each of us.

Before we made up our beds, Father went upstairs to see that everyone was OK and Sue came in to wish me good night. She looked gorgeous, with her hair down, and wearing a beautiful silk shimmering dressing gown. It nearly took my breath away. Holding her close to me was more blissful then I had ever imagined. We could have kissed all night through. She then said, "Sleep well mein Schatz (my darling) in your makeshift bed and I will see you in the morning."

Sue's father came back and we settled in our armchairs and talked for a while, mostly about my future, which was quite uncertain, and about his job as chief engineer at the hospital.

I wondered what kind of Christmas Eve my family was having at home without their two sons. They had written to me that they were well, except for my father. He had circulation problems and also problems with water retention. With all the hardships they had to endure, having barely enough food to go round, spending many hours in damp bomb shelters, no wonder their health was suffering. I wished I could talk to them. It was five years since my last Christmas at home with my family.

I finally fell asleep. The sleeping arrangements must have been very comfortable, because I didn't even hear Sue's father get up in the morning.

32

I was awakened by a tender kiss. As I opened my eyes I felt like a prince in fairyland. At first I didn't know where I was, until I saw Sue standing over me saying, "Good morning, Darling. Merry Christmas. Everyone is up already, you had better get up too." I reached up and pulled her face close to mine, kissing her and wishing her also a merry Christmas.

The two chairs her father had slept in were already back in their places. It didn't take me long to get dressed and washed and then I went to join the others.

The dining room table was set very festively. As I walked in, everybody wished me a merry Christmas. Sue's mother and father were busy in the kitchen preparing breakfast. I could smell eggs and bacon. Daisy, who was sitting next to me, leaned over and whispered, "We can open our gifts after breakfast." Sue came out of the kitchen with a plate full of toast, which had been fried in butter. It smelled delicious. A pan full of sliced and fried tomatoes followed this. Then her mother served fried eggs and some more toast.

Sue whispered to me, "This is my dad's favorite breakfast, I hope you like it." "Of course I will," I answered. After a year in the battlefields and nearly three years as a prisoner of war, it was like a king's table to me.

Pat and Daisy were first to finish their breakfast and asked if they could leave the table to open their gifts. However, they were told to wait until everyone was finished. After breakfast, we were all asked to go into the living room. It was a wonderful experience for me, to be part of the Christmas celebration in the circle of such a nice family.

We all gathered around the Christmas tree. I had secretly put my gifts underneath it with the rest of them. Pat was chosen to pick up the parcels from under the tree and hand them out. As it happened, I received the first present. It was a beautiful razor set from Sue and I was thrilled with it. She must have known that I needed one. Next came my gift for Daisy. When she saw it was a doll's cradle, hand made and hand painted, she was thrilled with it. Everyone was pleased with my gifts, which made me feel very good.

For Christmas dinner we had turkey and all the trimmings, followed by another glass of port wine. What a feast that was for me. I couldn't remember when I had last eaten such a delicious meal.

We all helped clear the table. Pat and Daisy showed us what they had learned in their ballet lessons. They were both very graceful. Then we sat and talked with Sue's parents. Her mother could not stress enough that I should go back to Germany to see my family. She said, "We love you very much Karl, but we want you to do what is best for you in the end."

I told them that I loved their daughter very much but realized I was only a prisoner of war. She was quick to correct me on that, "No Karl, you being a prisoner of war has nothing to do with it. To us, you are what you are as a person, and that is the only thing we see." It made me feel very good to hear that.

Sue reminded me that we intended to go for a walk to the place where I used to work. It was a cool but otherwise beautiful Christmas day, so Sue wore a coat and I borrowed one of her dad's cardigans.

I did not recognize the former building site. The large tree next to the old farmhouse, which was our shelter when it rained, was still there. The walkway, that Sue used to go on to her cousin's house, was gone. It was now a paved road, flanked by houses. We walked along the road until we came to a spot, about halfway down, where I stopped and said to Sue, "Well darling, judging by that group of trees over there, which they left standing, this is the spot where we first set eyes on each other." I took her into my arms and gave her a kiss.

Sue replied, "You know, Darling, this is the most important spot to me in the whole world."

"Yes dearest, if it wasn't for this spot, and if you hadn't picked up the very first note that I dropped here, we would never have got to know each other," I said. "What did you really see in me, a prisoner of war?"

"I don't really know," she answered. "All I know is that I liked you, but now I know that I love you." We held hands and walked around the place where our romance started.

For quite a while we didn't say anything more. We were both remembering the time when our love for each other began to grow. It was like a tender plant, which begins to grow in springtime but is so fragile that there is no guarantee it will survive the frost or the hail. However, the more difficulties we encountered, the stronger our love grew.

The afternoon was turning quite chilly. At the top of the new estate we found a barn belonging to a farmer. We went inside to get out of the cold and kissed some more. A tear rolled down Sue's cheek and she whispered, "Oh Karl, I don't want to think about tomorrow and I wish it would never come. Please tell me that you will always love me."

I answered, "Will you always love me, Darling?"

"Yes, I will always love you Karl, as long as I live," was her answer. When I told her it might be some time before we saw each other again, after I was sent back home to Germany, she kissed me and said, "I will wait for you my Darling."

It was getting dark as we left the barn and walked home, holding hands. Daisy ran to meet us saying that she had something to show me. She went upstairs to fetch the cradle I had given her with bedding, pillows, and a comforter in it, which her mother had sewn for her while we were gone. She also had a doll in it and she was obviously very pleased.

Supper was just about ready and we were both were hungry. After supper, Sue never left my side all evening. We all sat around a glowing fireplace and talked. The atmosphere was very cozy. Daisy played the piano, while Pat was ballet dancing. Grandma Cooper had been taken back home during the afternoon by Sue's father, so I was to sleep in the guest bedroom for the last night. It was agonizing for me to think that we might not see each other again for a long time.

Pat and Daisy went upstairs to bed and Sue's mother brought up the subject of my repatriation. She said, "I can't possibly imagine what it would be like not to see my family for five years." I told her that I was concerned about my father. The war years and concern for my brother and me must have taken their toll on his health.

When I returned to Germany about four months later, I learned that, when the French occupied our village, the French soldiers went from house to house, looking for young girls. My father managed to hide my two sisters in the attic of our house. He literally built a wall of bundled kindling wood around them in one corner. The French soldiers searched the attic, but did not find them. These and many more things must have been very worrying to my father.

By now everyone had retired for the night. While I was sitting in one of the armchairs, the door opened quietly and Sue came in to say good night. I motioned her to come and sit on my lap and soon she was in my arms, crying softly. We both realized that the end of my time as a prisoner of war in England was not too far away and there were no words to console us. After a while I said, "You had better go, Darling, before I keep you here all night." With that we got up and went upstairs to our rooms.

It felt like heaven sleeping in a real bed. I lay awake for a long time, reliving the whole weekend. The last thing I wanted to do was think about the next day. But then I remembered the words of Sue's mother; that I must be looking forward to seeing my family again after so many years. I guess I had to start thinking about that.

The night went by all too quickly. Unlike the day before, I woke up very early. I lay in bed, listening for sounds of people moving about, but I didn't hear anything and I didn't want to wake anyone, so I decided to just stay where I was. My train was not leaving till 1:30 p.m. so I had another full morning to spend with my darling Sue and her wonderful family. I had grown to like them all very much during these three days.

After about half an hour, I heard someone walking in the hallway and a gentle knock at my bedroom door. Sue came in and sat at my bedside. "I couldn't sleep any more, so I thought I would come and see you." I held her close to me and stroked her hair, which was falling over my face. We whispered softly for fear of waking anyone up.

Then she went to get dressed and soon I heard Pat and Daisy running in the hallway, chasing each other, and their mother telling them to be quiet.

By now everybody was up except me. Daisy called out, "Good morning Karl," and then ran away, giggling. It was time for me to get up and get ready. I came downstairs and made a point of saying "Good Morning" to Sue. She returned my greeting as if it was the first time we had seen each other.

I had a sausage and a fried egg for breakfast. Mother told us that we would have an early dinner, so that I could have a good meal before I left, and she was going to put up a couple of sandwiches for me to take on my trip.

After breakfast Sue and I went for a walk along Pasture Lane. We had a lot to talk about. I told Sue what a wonderful family she had and I hoped that one day I would be able to repay their kindness.

Time passed all too quickly. For a few moments we just gazed up into the sky. We watched the clouds drift by in front of the morning sun. They were changing color from white to pink and then to bright yellow.

Sue wanted to know if I ever had a girlfriend before. I answered, "Yes, I did have a girlfriend once, when I was 18, just before I joined the German air force. But she was nowhere near as beautiful as you are." Then I put my arms around her and gave her a long kiss, to put an end to her questions. I said, "I have never, nor will I ever, love anyone the way I love you, Darling."

We were beginning to feel cold so we went back to the house for a hot cup of tea. We all sat cozily around the fire, Sue very close to me holding my hand. Pat and Daisy wanted me to tell them another story so I told them a little about the place I grew up in.

"I lived in a small village, nestling among the hills, most of which were covered with large birch trees. Achalm was my favorite hill. On top of it stood a large ruined castle dating back to the 16th century. The path to it was still there which the knights had taken when they raided the surrounding villages. In the middle of the ruin stood a very tall tower, which was rebuilt in later years. The door to the tower was open and anyone who was not afraid of heights could get to the top via some wooden steps inside. On the way up, you could look through the openings, which were used by the knights to ward off enemy attacks with bow and arrows.

"As a boy, I used to love roaming the hills and mountains. Around Achalm there were meadows, where hundreds of sheep used to graze, watched by a shepherd. There were also huge chestnut trees, which I used to climb to gather the chestnuts and make baskets out of them for my sisters to play with. There were a lot of deer in the woods, which we liked to watch, especially at dusk when they came out onto the meadows to graze. Since we always carried a knife we would cut the best looking white thorn branches to make our own bows and arrows.

"During the winter I used to go to school on skates when the roads were icy, and on skis when there was a lot of snow. I made the skis from old wine barrels with the help of my older brother. In my later teens, I made my own skis from birch wood. I used to ski, hike and climb on every hill in and around our village.

"Most of the farmers in the village kept goats for milk. Every morning during the summer months, a young man, who was known as the goat herder, led the goats from the village onto the mountain meadows. He carried a horn, which he blew while walking through the streets early in the morning. All the farmer had to do was open the gate where the goats were kept and they would follow the goat herder. The boy would watch the goats while they grazed on the meadows all day. In the evening they would follow him home. When he walked through the village, the goats would go back to the places where they belonged, all by themselves."

It was soon time for dinner. We had a roast with gravy, potatoes, and a vegetable. It was superb, but Sue hardly ate anything. My appetite was not all that good either.

As soon as we had finished eating, Sue's father went to bring the car round to the front of the house. Sue's mother gave me a big hug, wishing me all the best for the future. I thanked her for her hospitality and said I hoped that we would meet again. Daisy wanted to know when I would come again. Sue explained that I had to go home to Germany first. Mother and the two girls all waved to me as we left.

Sue and I sat in the back seat. She held my hand very tight and was fighting back the tears. At the station we walked arm in arm to the waiting train. On the platform I put my arms around her. She was crying softly.

"If only we knew what the future held in store for us." I told her that as long as we didn't give up hope, the sun would shine for us again.

We kissed once more before I climbed the steps into the train. Sue held onto my hand until the train started to move. Once inside, I went to the nearest window and Sue walked along with the train until it picked up speed.

The train ride back to Peterborough seemed endless. I wanted to be back at my work in the post office, to take my mind off the last three days. Now I loved Sue more than ever. I longed to be in her arms, to feel her face, to look into her eyes, and to touch her tender lips with mine.

My dreams were interrupted when the conductor came into our compartment to check our tickets. He told me it would take another hour before we arrived in Peterborough.

After he left, the lady who sat opposite me started a conversation. She wanted to know where in Peterborough I was going to and told me that she and her husband owned a farm and had three of our boys working for them for quite some time. They were sorry to lose them when they were repatriated back to Germany. She didn't think they would ever get anybody again who worked so hard for them. I told her that I too had once worked for a farmer, but was now the mail orderly of the camp.

The time now passed much more quickly. The lady told me that her husband was coming to the station to pick her up, and if I needed a lift, they would gladly drop me off at the camp gate.

In Peterborough, when we got off the train, the lady offered to wait in case I wasn't picked up. However, I soon spotted our driver. On our thirty-minute drive to the camp he filled me in on everything that had happened at the camp during my absence.

He dropped me off outside my Nissen hut. I heard Struppie getting very excited inside. His greeting was the perfect welcome home.

The hut was cold, and so was the post office. First I had to bring in some wood and make a fire in my potbelly stove. It didn't take long before it felt comfortable. Struppie followed me very closely when I went to the kitchen for a cup of tea.

For quite some time after that wonderful holiday I had sleepless nights. I was afraid that our greatest wish, to be together forever, would never come true.

Sawtry, England

33

Life at the camp had changed so much since the beginning of 1948. With so many repatriations taking place, the number of prisoners in all the camps had shrunk. Some smaller camps had been completely dissolved and the prisoners moved into our camp. Rumors circulated for a while that our camp would be dissolved too and we would be moved to Sawtry, closer to Peterborough. The uncertainty made me very uneasy.

I did not see Jack for nearly two weeks after I got back, and I hoped that he had not been transferred to another camp. One morning he walked into my office. He had just returned from leave. He asked me if I noticed anything different about him. While looking him over, I noticed he had been promoted to sergeant, and congratulated him on his promotion.

The news I had from home was not very good. My sisters were very worried about my father's health. They also told me that one of our neighbors, who was also a prisoner of war in England and lived on the same street as us, had come home. They wondered when I would be released. Since my brother was reported missing, they were very much looking forward to having me back home. They also mentioned that our neighbor from across the street came home from a prison camp in Russia. He died just a week later.

The more I thought about it, the more I realized that the advice from Sue's mother, to go back to my loved ones, was the right thing to do.

Sue sent me a registered parcel and a letter. The parcel contained cigarettes, candy, and a tie. In her letter she told me that she was planning to come and visit me at Connington, together with her cousin Lorna, some time in early spring. She asked me to make inquiries about where they could stay for a week. I was thrilled that she was planning to come, but I would much prefer if she could come alone.

I decided to write a letter to Sue's parents. I thanked them for all the kindness they had shown me during my stay at their house and for the parcels they had sent to my family in Germany. Then I told them how I felt about their daughter and asked them to please let her come and visit me on her own. I made them a promise that I would never do anything, which they might disapprove of.

Next morning, Jack came into my office with a long list of names of all those to be repatriated from our camp. My name was not on it. He did not know what determined who went home, and who didn't, but he thought there was a good chance that I would be one of the last to go, probably in May. He was almost sure that he himself would be around until the very end. It depended entirely on the commander, as he was the one who made up the list.

With many men being transferred to our camp, and just as many leaving to go home, my work at the post office was hectic. Whenever we were not working, we were free to leave the confines of the camp and go wherever we wanted, as long as we signed out at the guardhouse, and signed back in before 10 p.m. All the restrictions about not being able to fraternize had been lifted completely.

Anyone who married a British subject could apply for permission to stay in England. There was a big article in the newspaper, which said that any English girl who married a German POW, no matter in which country they decided to live, could keep her British nationality. Sue was very quick to send that clipping for me to read.

Finally I received a letter from Sue in which she told me that she intended to visit me on her own, without her cousin, some time in April. She had made the arrangements with her employer and asked me to please find a family where she could stay. Her parents were very pleased with my letter and had no objections to her coming to see me. Now I had a lot to look forward to and plan for and we could talk about the future with a bit more certainty. Some of our men, especially those with no home to go to, had got married and stayed in England. Marrying Sue and staying here would have been an easier way out, but neither of us would have had any peace, wondering how my family was doing.

Extracts of a letter dated March 14th, 1948

My own dearest sweetheart Ursula,

Many thanks, my dear, for the lovely letter I received yesterday. I am so very happy that your parents were pleased with my letter and that they felt it was OK for you to come and visit me by yourself.

With every breath I breathe, I think of you and I can't begin to tell you how happy I feel, knowing that this spring time we will be able to spend a week together.

I learned from Jack that I will definitely be staying here at the camp till the end of April, hopefully even till May. We should have a most wonderful week together. I have befriended a nice family. They live not far from my office and they are willing to let you stay with them. They have had people staying with them before. The fee for bed and breakfast is very minimal. I could easily afford to pay it. There is even a possibility that you could have breakfast and any other meals with me at the sergeant's mess.

When you say in your letter that you saw some of our boys walking through the streets of Bradford, you can't imagine how terrible it makes me feel, knowing that, if I was there now, I would be able to see you almost every day. However things have worked out better for us than I ever imagined.

I would like nothing better than to spend Easter with you and your family. However, the way things are at the moment, I don't think they would let me go. Please remember My Darling that wherever I go, I will carry you along in my heart. You are in my thoughts every minute of my days and before I go to sleep. You are in my dreams, and the very first thought that comes to my mind when I wake up in the mornings, is you. You are everything to me.

Well darling, the mail has now arrived and I must get busy sorting, and deliver it. I'll say bye, bye till my next letter.

I love and adore you with all my heart and remain with lots of kisses Yours Karl.

I waited anxiously for a reply from Sue. The first thing I did every day was to search through the mail for a letter from her. More and more men were being repatriated. One time we were down to around 500 men.

There were still rumors about being moved to another camp.

Whenever I had a chance, I took Struppie for a walk through the farmland. I just loved the springtime. Everything was so lush and green. Struppie had fun trying to chase the colorful dragonflies every time we passed the pond where we sat with Sue and her family the previous summer.

Walking with Struppie reminded me that very soon I would have to look for someone who would give him a good home. I had grown to like him so much that I knew I was going to miss him very much when I had to let him go. I kept thinking that he must have come from a farm or a house from this neighborhood when he first appeared on the doorstep of my office. However, among the many people I met while walking Struppie, no one ever said that they had seen him before. One thing was for sure; I could not just leave him there. I wanted him to have a good home. I could picture him sitting in front of my empty Nissen hut, fretting for me after I had left.

One morning the camp commander (major) came to my office and spent nearly half an hour with me. He said that it looked as if we would be staying at our camp till at least the end of April. Then those of us who were still here would all be repatriated and the camp would be closed down. He was going to write a memo to our German commander to let everyone know. The Sawtry camp would be shut down and absorbed by us, so we would be almost a thousand men again, and I would have my hands full with the extra mail. However, with the pending repatriations there was nowhere near the volume of mail that there used to be. I myself had already told my people in Germany not to write any more.

That evening I needed to go for a walk. I wanted to remember the time when I first met Sue and I wanted to think about the future. Seeing the spring flowers and the beautiful green meadows uplifted me as they had done so many times before. I could see myself being married to Sue, although the word marriage had never come up in our conversations so far.

While I was meditating and enjoying the scenery, a farmer came walking by, who I had seen before when Sue and I were sitting in the same spot. I started a conversation with him. He wanted to know who Struppie belonged to. I answered that he had been my faithful companion for almost two years and that, since I was to be repatriated in about a month's time, I was hoping to find a good home for him. The farmer bent down to stroke Struppie, who first growled at him and then accepted his friendship by wagging his tail.

The farmer pointed out his farm to me, just across the fields. He said that his wife would probably like to have Struppie as a companion around the farm, and he could do with a good rat catcher. We arranged for the farmer and his wife to come by one evening so that she could have a look at Struppie.

The next day there was a letter for me from Sue, telling me that she was planning to be in Connington by the 17th of April, one day after my birthday and she would be staying for one week. I was relieved to know we would see each other again before I left.

Struppie and I went for a long walk. I wanted the farmer's wife to meet with him and I wanted him to see his future home.

As we approached the farm, Struppie became very alert and excited. Since I was not sure what animals might be running loose, I put him on his lead. The first thing I noticed was that everything was very clean and well kept. I rang the doorbell. Evidently there was no dog, otherwise it would have announced our arrival.

When the front door opened the lady seemed pleased to see us. To my amazement, Struppie did not growl at her and accepted being stroked without a murmur. The farmer's wife told me that her husband was in the field but if I had the time she would gladly make a cup of tea for me.

We sat down at the table to talk about Struppie. I told her that I was very relieved to know she was willing to take care of him. I asked her about the other animals on the farm. She said there were some cats, which lived in the barns, but they were not domesticated and very shy. She didn't think there would be any problems with Struppie.

While we were enjoying the tea and biscuits, Struppie made himself very much at home, lying under the table. I told the lady that I would like to keep him until my repatriation.

Everything was turning out so well, but I couldn't wait to see Sue again and the days in the camp sometimes seemed endless. Though I was busy in the post office, my mind was mainly occupied with two things. One was Sue's forthcoming visit; the other was preparing myself to go home to my family and the village where I was born.

I knew it was going to be different from six years ago, when I left as a young air force volunteer. Now I was going back to a country occupied by French forces, and devastated by six years of war. I didn't know what to expect or even what I was going to do. I hoped that the company, where I had served my apprenticeship, was still operating. Even if it wasn't, I had a good profession and the prospect of finding work was not too remote.

About three days before Sue's arrival I received a beautiful hand-painted birthday card from her. I had forgotten that my 24th birthday was only two days away, my third birthday in captivity. She also wrote that she would be coming by bus from Peterborough, and it would drop her off outside the camp gate.

That evening I went into the British orderly room and asked if I could make a phone call to my girlfriend. Sue's parents did not have a telephone, but their neighbors did, and they had once told Sue that they would be willing to fetch her to the phone if I needed to call her. One of the orderlies dialed the number for me and finally Sue was on the other end of the line. She was as nervous as I was and could hardly speak. I just managed to tell her that I had received her letter, I loved her, and that I would be waiting for her at the camp gate when she arrived.

I awoke very early on April 17th 1948. The weather forecast was good. I had lain my trousers underneath my bed sheet overnight, a trick I had learned during my air force days. With my body heat and weight, the trousers got somewhat pressed. I had a freshly washed shirt to put on and my shoes were polished. Everything was set and my heart was racing.

I went earlier than usual to pick up the mail as I would need to have everything ready and delivered by two.

Jack came into my office at around nine o'clock to help me sort the mail. Then he took all the mail belonging to the British staff and said he would take care of it. What a good friend he was.

I had finished my work before noon, which gave me plenty of time to prepare myself. Everyone I met called out to me to have fun. It seemed half the British staff knew about Sue's visit and probably half of Connington too.

34

Two o'clock came quickly. I left to walk down to the guardhouse and Struppie wanted to come along. I told him that I would be back soon and he seemed to understand. I went in to chat with the guard and very soon a taxi pulled up and Sue got out.

I ran to her and we embraced, right there in front of the guardhouse. I kissed her like I had never kissed her before. Sue said, "Oh Karl, I just couldn't wait for a bus; I had to get here as fast as I could. I do love you Karl and my parents love you too, that's why they let me come."

Finally we went to my place for a cup of tea. As we walked past the guardhouse the guard grinned and waved to us. Sue started giving me greetings from everyone, especially from her parents and sisters.

When we arrived at my hut, Struppie went frantic. He chased round and round Sue, stopping every so often to be patted by her. Sue was pleased that I had found a good home for him.

As soon as he had settled down, Sue and I were in each other's arms again. When I told her that I was thinking of staying in England she said, "Please don't Karl, I love you enough to wait, however long it takes."

I kissed her passionately and held her as close as I possibly could and said, "Oh Darling, I just don't want to leave you behind, I am afraid of losing you."

There was a tear in her eye when she said, "You know Karl, it is going to be very hard for me too to see you go, but please don't be afraid of losing me. I love you too much to let anything come between us. Please promise me that you will never ever think like that again." I kissed her again and promised that I wouldn't. Tears rolled down her face again and I gently wiped them away.

Then Sue opened her case and handed me some gifts. There were cigarettes and goodies that her mother sent along for me. Sue had bought me a beautiful fountain pen, for writing with after I returned home. There was also a card from Daisy and Pat, wishing me all the best for the future, and to come back soon.

We were getting hungry and I still hadn't managed to get the cup of tea I had promised her. She preferred to stay with Struppie, while I went over to the canteen. The boys there offered to make us both a sandwich and as much tea as we needed, providing I brought Sue over to see them some time. I promised that I would.

When I got back, Sue was having fun with Struppie. I was given a sausage for him and I made him sit up and beg for it. It kept him quiet for a while. Sue held my hand and said, "Oh Karl, I hope it will not be too long before we can share every minute of our life together like this."

I hugged her and said, "Because we love each other the way we do, I know that day will come."

The tea and the sandwich tasted good and the afternoon went by swiftly.

We walked down the lane to the house where Sue would be staying, talking of the experiences we had at Clayton and the Westfield camp, the beginning of our courting days, if you could call it that. Sometimes we didn't see each other for weeks and then, if we were lucky, spent a few moments talking through barbed wire. An unusual courtship.

The lady was expecting us. She lived alone and was glad of the company. I introduced Sue as my fiancée, and soon realized that the two of them would get along fine together.

Sue's bedroom was very roomy and had a pleasant atmosphere. The lady told us that she would make breakfast between 7:00 and 9:00 a.m. Also she gave her a key and said she could come and go whenever she pleased. She herself was going to be there most of the time. We thanked the lady and said that Sue would look forward to seeing her at breakfast the next morning.

We picked up Struppie and took him for a walk to our favorite pond, and I was able to point out to Sue where Struppie was going to live after I had gone back to Germany.

We could not have wished for a nicer spring evening, with the fragrance of spring flowers in the air and the birds singing their evening song. We watched a pair of blue tits making their nest, flying busily back and forth and feeding on insects and green caterpillars.

At the pond we saw more dragonflies than ever before. They seemed to perform their evening dance just for us. Their wings reflected every color in the evening sun. We sat down to admire their ballet performance and mating dance.

Slowly I turned towards my sweetheart to embrace her. She whispered, "Oh Karl, I love you so much, with all my heart and my whole being." As I held her close to me I had great difficulty controlling my feelings. I wanted to hold her closer than ever before. I held her face in my hands, looked deep into her beautiful eyes and whispered that we had to keep the promise I made to her parents.

She agreed, "Yes Karl, we will continue to love each other until the day when we shall be as one."

Suddenly Sue asked, "You introduced me as your fiancée Karl; does that mean that we are engaged?"

Immediately I knelt down before her and said, "I would like to ask the young lady for her hand, to be married at some later date. I don't have a ring to give you, but I give you my promise to be always true to you, not sharing my heart with anyone until the day that we shall be joined in marriage."

Tears of joy rolled down her face as she said, "Oh Karl, I do love you without a ring."

We kissed and I whispered softly, "Darling, we are now engaged."

We sat and watched the dance of the dragonflies a little longer and Sue said, "What a beautiful engagement, thank you Karl."

The sun had set. Arm in arm we walked slowly back and all the fears that I once had about leaving Sue behind had vanished.

Back at the Nissen hut, I made us a cup of tea, to celebrate our engagement. For the rest of the evening we sat on my bed talking, hugging and kissing. It was wonderful just being together. Sue told me how good it felt being my fiancée, even without a ring, and that having me was the most beautiful engagement present she could wish for.

We were surprised to see that it was almost ten o'clock. I walked Sue home to her bed and breakfast place. On the way I told her that I hoped to be through with the mail by around eleven o'clock the next day, then we could take a bus into Peterborough and watch a movie. She thought that was a good idea.

The light at the house was still on and the lady called out to wish us a good night. I kissed Sue good night and went back to my hut.

I lay down to sleep, imagining Sue lying beside me. I relived our engagement and the wonderful moments we had together. Before long I was asleep.

The next day started out very dreary and rainy and a lot cooler. I went for breakfast early, where I heard that another 50 of our men were to be repatriated. I wondered when my time would come. I also picked the mail up early. To my biggest surprise there was a letter for Sue, in her mother's handwriting. There was not much mail, but it was enough to keep me busy all morning.

Jack paid me a visit at the office, asking about Sue. When I told him that we became engaged while sitting at the pond he felt privileged to be the first to congratulate me. He helped me to get my work finished early and then offered to give us a ride into Peterborough, as he had some business to take care of there.

It was almost 12 o'clock when Struppie started wagging his tail and watching the door. Before I could ask him what was up, the door opened and Sue walked in, looking as beautiful as ever. She fell into my arms and kissed me good morning. She was most surprised when I delivered her the letter from her mother. I told her that in the days before we were allowed to receive any mail, I always used to pick out her letters first. She let me read her mother's letter and I couldn't help but notice her concern for her daughter. She also wished us both a wonderful time together, and reminded me that very soon I would be back in my homeland and united with my loved ones.

Jack arrived to pick us up and greeted Sue with, "Welcome my beautiful lady, I hope you don't mind riding in a Land Rover." We all squeezed into the front seat together and he dropped us off in Peterborough.

Being alone with Sue in a city, I felt like a free man. We enjoyed strolling around the city, looking in shop windows. We looked for the bus stop and found out that a bus was leaving for Connington every half an hour.

Several movies were showing at the cinema. Sue chose to see *When the bough breaks,* a love story. There was a long line of people waiting to get in and we sat in a full house. Like most of the couples, I put my arm around Sue. It felt good to be able to act like anyone else. During the film I kissed Sue occasionally. We enjoyed the love story but I was disappointed that it had a sad ending. Throughout the movie I held Sue's hand. We would send love signals by squeezing each other's hands.

We caught the bus back to camp and went to find out what was cooking at the sergeants' mess. It was roast beef and Yorkshire pudding, a real treat.

The evening was cool, but we always enjoyed a walk. We went along the road leading to Wansford. The fragrance of wild clematis, which lined the side of the road, filled the air. Every so often we would stop to embrace and kiss, not wanting to think about having to part again.

The rest of the week went by all too quickly. Sue's last day started dreary and miserable. I had no appetite for breakfast and sat waiting for Sue to come. All of a sudden I realized that she had a suitcase and that I should be helping her to bring it here. I walked down to the house and found Sue and her landlady having a little breakfast. I was invited to join them. Like magic I cheered up when she said, "You sure make a fine couple and you have so much to look forward to." After breakfast we sat and talked a little and then said good-bye to the lady and thanked her for her hospitality.

Jack was his usual cheery self when he came to pick us up and brought greetings from his fiancée. Sue said good-bye to Struppie, telling him that she loved him very much. He wagged his tail and seemed to understand.

The ride to the station was very quiet. We did not know when we would see each other again. Sue lay her head on my shoulder, choking back the tears and whispering to me that she loved me.

Jack said good-bye to Sue and told me he would wait outside the station.

The train was waiting at the platform. I helped Sue to put her suitcase into a compartment and put the window down for her. Then we waited outside until the last minute. The conductor called out, "All aboard," and blew his whistle.

Sue and I said at the same time, "I love you."

When she was in her compartment I held her hand with both of mine. Tears were rolling down her face. I walked along with the train as far as I could, holding onto her hand. Finally I had to let go as the train picked up speed and carried her swiftly away.

For some time I stood motionless, gazing in the direction of the train.

Then I remembered Jack, waiting to take me back, and hurried out of the station. Jack offered to treat me to some Chinese food. He said he was hungry and knew a place where they cooked very well. We pulled up in front of a fine restaurant. I had chow mein with glazed chicken and rice and Jack had beef and chicken. We sat and talked about the future of the camp. He didn't know where he would go after the camp was dissolved. He had another year left in the army and he wasn't sure if he would sign on for a few more years after that.

Back at the camp, Struppie was looking for Sue when I entered my Nissen hut. I patted him and told him that she was gone. There was very little to do at the post office, so I sat down to write a letter to Sue.

35

Two days later we were all asked to line up for roll call. We were informed that the complete repatriation of the camp would take place in three stages. All the names were read out and my name came up in the last stage, which was to be on April 30th, just six days away. The last mailing was to be in two days time. I was glad that finally we knew where we stood and could prepare ourselves to go home.

The next morning Jack came to see me at the office. He had been assigned to stay until all of us were gone. Most of his comrades would be going to different assignments around the country and some would be discharged.

After I had delivered the last of the mail, my duty as mail orderly was completed and I met Jack at the sergeants' mess for lunch. The boys in the kitchen told me that they hoped I would come and eat there every day until my repatriation.

When I got back to my hut I put Struppie's lead on him and we walked to the farm, which would be his new home. As we passed our favorite pond, I had to stop and sit down and remember the last time I sat there with Sue, the day I asked for her hand in marriage. I thought how strange life was. Here I was in an enemy country, not wanting to leave it, and realizing that there were so many good people everywhere.

I had plenty of time, so I decided to play with Struppie one last time and give him some affection. I knew I was going to miss him very much and I felt I needed some affection too. I took another good look at our favorite dragonfly pond, wishing that I had a camera to capture these wonderful memories. Then we strolled through the fields to Struppie's new home.

The farmer's wife was busy in the garden. She saw us coming and waved. As we got closer I took Struppie off the lead. The lady called him by his name and he ran towards her as if he had always known her. She invited me in but I declined as I had plenty to do to get everything ready. I asked her to put Struppie on the leash until I was out of sight. I didn't want him to run after me. Then I told him that I was going to leave him and that he had to be a good boy for the lady. I hugged him once more and turned for home. When I looked back I saw him going into the house.

The next three days were occupied with packing and getting ready for the first leg of our repatriation. We were told that we would be traveling by train to London and then to a transit camp somewhere in the south of England. I had quite a few clothes, which my tailor friend had made me, and also a couple of plants that were my prize possession.

On our last day we visited with old friends and exchanged addresses. I received a parcel from Sue, containing a few packets of cigarettes, some candies, and other goodies, which would come in handy while traveling.

Best of all, the boys in the orderly room put me through to Sue's neighbors on the phone, and Sue and I talked together for a few minutes.

On the morning of April 30th the final 400 men were all lined up, with two officers and two corporals to accompany us. Some of us had to open our kit bags for inspection before we were put on large military trucks to be taken to the railway station.

A special train was waiting to take us to London. The ride was very unpleasant. We were cramped together like flies, many had to stand all the way, and on top of that it was an unusually hot day. We were issued one sandwich and nothing to drink. The ride took all day and I was very glad when we arrived in London.

At around 5:30 p.m. we were unloaded and taken to a large hall. It reminded me so much of the day we arrived in London three years ago. This time, however, we were not stripped naked. Instead, we were physically examined by a doctor, then fingerprinted and handed our release document. We were told to keep this paper with us at all times.

The same evening we were all transported via underground to Bury St. Edmunds. We had to walk to the transit camp and the weight of our kit bags (about 50 pounds) made us all tired and weary. The conditions in the camp were similar to three years ago. Over 100 of us were packed into one hut. We had to sleep on the floor, or wherever there was room to lie down. I thought longingly of my Nissen hut at Connington, a palace compared to this.

But it was only to be for fourteen days. The food was awful and not enough and I longed for Sue. I found out the exact address of the camp so that she could write to me.

The address was: # 186 POW Base Camp, Farnham Park, Nr. Bury St. Edmunds, Serial. # 342 / No. of hut # 134,
Suffolk.

My first letter to Sue was full of complaints. I just wasn't used to living like a POW any more. Most of the men sat around all day doing nothing but playing cards. I kept to myself. My only thought all day was of the sweetheart I had left behind.

After about a week I received a letter from Sue. She told me how much she missed me and she hoped and prayed that I was all right. On her trip back to Bradford she couldn't stop crying. Her world felt like it had come to an end.

Camp life was very boring. The nights were the worst because the weather had turned unseasonally hot. Being cooped up in those wooden barracks was a nightmare for us all. We had worked on English farms, building sites, coalmines and brickyards for three years, and now we were being shoved off. Maybe they wanted us to feel that we had lost the war.

Finally the day came to leave. On May 16th, about 1000 men were taken by train to Harwich, to be loaded onto a troop transport ship. The weather was beautiful, which indicated a good crossing.

At noon we set out across the Channel, away from beautiful England. I had grown to love its people and the further we sailed away the heavier my heart became. I said a silent good-bye to the disappearing coastline.

After an hour at sea the weather suddenly changed. Huge waves lapped the boat and almost everyone became seasick. The ship had three decks. I happened to be on the second one. The men on the third deck were hanging over the railing vomiting. The green juice from their stomachs came raining down on us, standing at the railings below, hoping the air would make us feel better. Instead it made us feel worse.

We were on the water for eight hours. When we finally arrived at the Hoek of Holland at 8:00 p.m. that evening, we were worn out.

Four hours later we were on a train taking us through Holland into Germany. That night I was so tired that I just slid down where I was standing in the crowded train and tried to get some rest.

When we finally arrived, we found ourselves near Hanover, in the transit camp of Munster-Lager. Some of us slept in tents, while others, including myself, found shelter in wooden barracks. I was so tired and weary that I slept for a whole day without any food. When I woke up, I found out that the food was even worse than in England. Things were getting worse rather than better. The camp was packed with about 1000 men.

We were told that it would take six to eight days until we would continue our trip to our respective areas, either American, British, French or Russian occupied zones. The next six days were hell. We were hardly given anything to eat or drink. No one was allowed to leave the camp.

On May 24th I was on a train going south towards the French zone. By now I didn't much care what happened. I was glad that Sue didn't know where I was. She would probably think that I was at home with my family. I had asked her to write to my home address so that I would have a letter by the time I got there.

After about five hours we finally reached Bad Kreuznach, not far from the city I had to report to when I joined the German air force as an 18-year-old. I had made a six-year circle around different parts of the world and ended up at the same place where I had started out. I was about two hours from home.

As the train slowly rolled into the station I could hardly believe my eyes. There were about 50 French soldiers lining the platform with bayonets on their rifles. I thought we were supposed to be released and now we were being taken prisoner all over again. There were only a handful of British soldiers accompanying thousands of us, and now half the French army seemed to be taking over.

After getting off the train we were lined up and marched to our new camp, flanked by the French soldiers. We were treated like a new lot of prisoners.

The next day we were physically examined. They were mainly looking for a stamp under our arms. During the war, all the men belonging to an SS unit had their blood group permanently branded into their skin. It could not be erased except by surgery. This was done in case they received any injuries in battle which required blood, to find out what type of blood the injured man needed. It was not practiced in any other unit except the SS. All those who were found with such a mark were sent to France to work in their coalmines, three years after the war had ended. Again I was glad of the decision I had made to join the paratroopers instead of the SS.

Four more days in the POW camp, which seemed more like four years, and I was released. There were about 30 of us lined up in front of the camp gate. We were each given a voucher for sandwiches, which constituted our food ration until we got home. In my pocket I carried my certificate of discharge, which entitled me to ride the train to the city of Reutlingen, which was about four miles from my village.

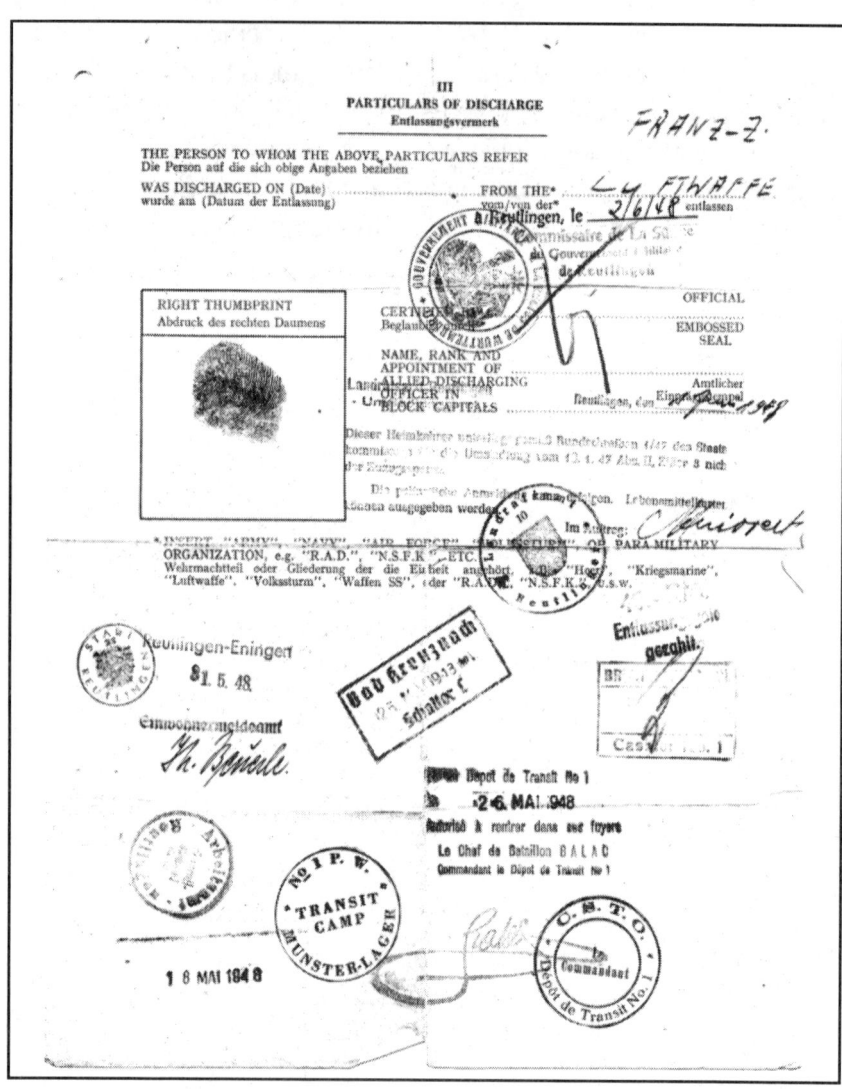

My final release papers (front)

FRANZ-2

CONTROL FORM D.2
Kontrollblatt D.2

CERTIFICATE OF DISCHARGE
Entlassungschein

ALL ENTRIES WILL BE MADE IN BLOCK LATIN CAPITALS AND WILL BE MADE IN INK OR TYPE-SCRIPT.	**I** **PERSONAL PARTICULARS** Personalbeschreibung	Dieses Blatt muss in folgender weise ausgefüllt werden: 1. In lateinischer Druckschrift und in grossen Buchstaben. 2. Mit Tinte oder mit Schreibmaschine.

SURNAME OF HOLDER ... **KERN**
Familienname des Inhabers

DATE OF BIRTH ... **16.4.24.**
Geburtsdatum (DAY/MONTH/YEAR)

CHRISTIAN NAMES ... **KARL**
Vornamen des Inhabers

PLACE OF BIRTH ... **EWINGEN**
Geburtsort

CIVIL OCCUPATION ... **TÜRNER**
Beruf oder Beschäftigung

FAMILY STATUS—SINGLE † Ledig
Familienstand   MARRIED   Verheiratet
WIDOW(ER)   Verwitwet
DIVORCED   Geschieden

HOME ADDRESS Strasse **METZINGER STR. 3**
Heimatanschrift Ort ... **EWINGEN**
Kreis ... **REUTLINGEN**
Regierungsbezirk and ... **WÜRTTB.**

NUMBER OF CHILDREN WHO ARE MINORS
Zahl der minderjährigen Kinder ...

I HEREBY CERTIFY THAT TO THE BEST OF MY KNOWLEDGE AND BELIEF THE PARTICULARS GIVEN ABOVE ARE TRUE. I ALSO CERTIFY THAT I HAVE READ AND UNDERSTOOD THE "INSTRUCTIONS TO PERSONNEL ON DISCHARGE" (CONTROL FORM D.1).
SIGNATURE OF HOLDER ... **Kern Karl**
Unterschrift des Inhabers

Ich erkläre hiermit, nach bestem Wissen und Gewissen, dass die obigen Angaben wahr sind. Ich bestätige ausserdem dass ich die "Anweisung für Soldaten und angehörige militärähnlicher Organisationen" u.s.w. (Kontrollblatt D.1) gelesen und verstanden habe.

II
MEDICAL CERTIFICATE
Ärztlicher Befund

DISTINGUISHING MARKS ...
Besondere Kennzeichen

DISABILITY, WITH DESCRIPTION ...
Dienstunfähigkeit, mit Beschreibung

MEDICAL CATEGORY ... **FIT**
Tauglichkeitsgrad

I CERTIFY THAT TO THE BEST OF MY KNOWLEDGE AND I LIEF THE ABOVE PARTICULARS RELATING TO THE HOLDER ARE TRUE AND THAT HE IS NOT VERMINOUS OR SUFFERING FROM ANY INFECTIOUS OR CONTAGIOUS DISEASE.

Ich erkläre hiermit, nach bestem Wissen und Gewissen, dass die obigen Angaben wahr sind, dass der Inhaber ungezieferfrei ist und dass er keinerlei ansteckende oder übertragbare Krankheit hat.

SIGNATURE OF MEDICAL OFFICER ...
Unterschrift des Sanitätsoffiziers

NAME AND RANK OF MEDICAL OFFICER IN BLOCK LATIN CAPITALS ... **Dr. Kurt Engelke**
Zuname/Vorname/Dienstgrad des Sanitätsoffiziers
(In lateinischer Druckschrift und in grossen Buchstaben)

P.T.O.
Bitte wenden

† DELETE THAT WHICH IS INAPPLICABLE
Nichtzutreffendes durchstreichen

My final release papers (back)

Eningen, Germany

36

At about 9:00 a.m. on May 30th 1948 I finally looked freedom in the eye. I could hardly believe it. For the first time in three years there were no guards, no barbed wire, no one to tell me what to do. I was free, free, free. My first reaction was to run. I ran as fast as my legs could carry me for fear my captors would change their minds. I didn't look back but ran until I was sure that I was out of sight.

When I came to a main road I stopped. I had the address of the place where we were to pick up our rations, but I had no idea how far it was. At that moment I saw a large truck approaching and decided to flag it down. To my surprise the driver stopped.

When I asked for a ride into town, he motioned me to jump onto the empty flatbed trailer. First I threw on my bag and then jumped on myself. Immediately the driver took off. He drove very fast, as if he wanted to make up for lost time. Since the trailer was empty and the road was badly in need of repair, I was tossed up and down. Desperately I tried to find something to hold onto because I was afraid of being thrown under the wheels. The only chance I had was to hang onto the side with one hand, while holding my kit bag with the other. After a terrifying 20 minutes we finally halted in the city and I found myself standing alone in the street.

About 30 yards away there was a line of men who looked like me, carrying kit bags and standing outside a house. I walked over, found that I was at the right place and also stood in line. Once inside, I showed my voucher and my release papers and was handed two sandwiches in a brown paper sack. Before leaving I asked for directions to the railroad station and was told to leave by the back door.

Outside I found a shocking sight. About twenty or thirty people, both young and old, and mothers with their children, were begging for food. My pity fell especially on a mother sitting at the roadside with three young children around her. I reached into my paper sack and gave her one and a half of my sandwiches. Since I didn't know how long it would take to get home, nor how much food they would have when I got there, I kept half a sandwich for myself.

At the train station I saw a similar picture, mothers and children sitting around the station hall, begging for food and cigarettes. Almost anyone would exchange cigarettes for food.

Before long I was on my last train ride home. My feelings were mixed. I was free, yet I was going to have to find a place in a society that was no longer like the one I had known six years ago. It was a country struggling with poverty and trying to recover from a very destructive war. There was rubble lying around the bombed-out streets. Much of the city had been totally destroyed.

The train station had also been damaged. I walked to the tram stop, which I used to use during the winter months to travel to college and to work. While I was waiting for the tram I hoped that I might see someone I knew. Many people from Eningen used the tram to go back and forth to work and for shopping in the city. But I only saw young people, who were too young to know me, and old ones who were too busy to take notice of someone standing there with a kit bag. I saw no one who knew me.

A quarter of an hour later I got off the tram in the village of Eningen-unter-Achalm. My heart was sad. I felt like a stranger. For a while I stood and looked around. Almost everything still looked the way it had when I left six years earlier. I threw my bag onto my shoulder and made my way towards our house.

The road was very familiar. Very close to the tram stop was the school I used to attend. Then I noticed that the old fountain, where I used to stop on the way to school to wet my sponge, was still running. I passed the little corner shop, which sold candies and post cards. Then came the house of a school friend of mine with whom I used to do my homework and play cards. I wondered if he had made it back after the war. I knew practically every house and every detail of this road because I had walked it a thousand times before. I came to a corner of the street from which I could see the house in which I was born, and where I hoped to find my family. No one knew when I would be coming home.

I saw my middle sister, Gertrud, coming from the garden shed with a basket, and called out, "Trudel!" First she looked bewildered; then she recognized me, dropped the basket and ran towards me. We hugged each other and cried with joy. Then she ran ahead to announce my arrival to the rest of the family.

My father came out to greet me, followed by my younger sister Anny. We had a very emotional reunion. My eldest sister, Luise, was married and living in another city. My elder brother, Walter, was missing in Russia. The four of us now made up the Kern family.

After so many years of separation we had a lot to tell each other. My sisters told me the names of all my school friends and neighbors who did not make it back after the war. Then they wanted to know all about the girl called Ursula, how I came to meet her, what she looked like and how she felt when I left her behind. They all thought what a wonderful family she must have to send them parcels and letters. I said I was very much in love with her. Anny smiled and took something out from behind her back. It was a long letter from Sue. It had arrived a few days earlier and then my family knew that it would not be long before I was home.

Before I opened the letter, I showed them a photo of Sue, a small picture of her standing in the garden. They all thought she looked very beautiful. Since I had only been home a few hours, I could not bring myself to tell them that I was planning to go back to England.

Sue's letter made me feel very heartsick. I missed her terribly and I had no idea how I was going to get back to England. I decided that I would stay home for a week or so to gradually settle down to civilian status. My father was 62 years old and the only breadwinner in the family.

There were also many things I had to take care of. One of them was to report to the town hall to be registered. My family told me I gave them a scare when I was reported killed in action.

I did not sleep well at nights so I made an appointment with the doctor. Eventually he came to the conclusion that all the years of stress from the war and prison camps had taken their toll on my health.

Two weeks after I returned home, I went into Reutlingen to look up the company where I had served my apprenticeship. To my biggest surprise, I was told that I could start work as a tool and die maker in a week's time.

Things were looking a little better and I was feeling much more optimistic about the future. I was happy to be earning and helping to support the family.

Every week I received one or even two letters from my darling Sue. I answered them all diligently. I had to tell her that the conditions in Germany were worse than I had expected. However I was thrilled to let her know that I was working for my old company and was trying my best to save up for my fare back to England.

But by the time I helped to pay for the extra food there was very little left to save. Some of the food I had to obtain on the black market. My father's health was worsening, although he would not admit it. Weeks and months went by without me getting any closer to fulfilling my dream of going back to England.

Shortly before Christmas a big parcel of food arrived from Sue's parents. Since we were not farmers it was extremely difficult for us to get hold of any meat. Our company manufactured wire production machines, which were used to make nails, barbed wire and chain-link fences. Besides being paid with money, we also received a few pounds of nails each payday. Farmers would give a lot of meat for a few nails, so many of my evenings were occupied in finding connections for food.

While serving in the air force I had received a salary and had accumulated a tidy sum in the bank. However, money was so devalued that it wouldn't even buy me a pair of socks. I had to wear my brother's suits as my own clothes were too small for me.

My job at the company was going well, there was plenty of work and I earned good money. If only I could have saved more. Unfortunately it looked as if my father would have to give up working.

In the meantime Sue had gone into children's nursing. Her mother thought it would be a good way for her to be occupied. I kept her informed about everything that happened in our family and that I wasn't able to come back to England as quickly as we thought.

It was a very quiet Christmas. The biggest joy for all of us was that I could spend it with my family. During the war and as a prisoner of war I used to dream of being home for Christmas. Now that it finally materialized, it was not the way I had pictured it.

37

Spring and summer went by and I was getting very lovesick for my darling. It was my father who suggested that perhaps she could come to Germany.

To my biggest surprise, Sue wrote that she had already applied for a passport and that she was determined to come for a visit. Many of her relatives took a dim view of her plans but her parents were not against it. She was booked on a flight to Frankfurt in the middle of September.

About one week before her arrival I started getting heart trouble symptoms and problems with dizziness. Four days later I was in hospital. Now I was really worried. I had planned to go to Frankfurt by train and meet Sue at the airport.

My only means of transportation was a motorbike. My sister Gertrud offered to go to Frankfurt to meet Sue. However, since she could not speak any English, nor Sue any German, we decided it would make more sense to hire a taxi to pick her up. It was a good three-and-a-half hour's drive from Eningen to Frankfurt. We found a man who was willing to drive there and back for a reasonable price. To be able to pay him I had to sell my motorcycle.

While in hospital I underwent several tests, including ECGs. No one was sure what the problem was but it was definitely not my heart. The day before my sister was due to go to Frankfurt I had a talk with the doctor about my release. He told me that they were planning to do some more tests on me. So I told him that if I were not released the next day, I would walk out of the hospital of my own accord.

The next morning I was released. I was determined to be at home when Sue arrived. We had two large bedrooms and a very large living room. Sue was to sleep in the bedroom with my two sisters. There was a single bed for Sue and my sisters slept in a large queen-size bed.

Very late at night I heard the Volkswagen beetle drive up in front of our house. They had arrived. Quickly I went down to meet them. My heart was beating so fast that I thought it would jump out of my chest. Soon we were in one another's arms. Sue said, "Oh Karl, I am so glad you are all right. Your sister tried to tell me so many things but I couldn't make out what was happening. I had an idea that you must be ill."

I kissed her and told her that I was all right and explained that I was in hospital until this morning. "Now you are here, I know that I am going to be OK."

The next hours were filled with talking, translating, and explaining. Except for a little turbulence, Sue had had a good flight. There were no jets on domestic flights in those days; she came in a small prop airplane.

My sisters had made a very good soup, which we all enjoyed. I suggested Sue send a telegram home first thing in the morning to let her parents know that she had arrived safely. However, they had stopped on the way from Frankfurt and already sent one. Gertrud understood the word telegram because it is the same in German. So that was taken care of.

I was fast asleep one night when one of my sisters came to wake me up. Sue's bed cover kept slipping onto the floor. I realized that Sue did not know how to sleep under a feather quilt because they didn't have them in England. When feather beds are made in the morning the feathers are shaken down and the rest of the cover is folded under. However, before getting into bed it is opened up and shaken so that the feathers are equally distributed. My sisters apologized for not telling her, we all had a good laugh and went back to sleep.

Similar occurrences happened every day. My Sue was a quick learner and each day she learned something new.

I was off work with a doctor's note for almost a month and the union paid my wages. This gave me a chance to show Sue around the village. We went for walks in the woods and she got to know the place I grew up in. The people in the village grew to love Sue very much. They liked her openhearted nature and they were fascinated when she tried to speak Swabian, our local dialect.

Sue's visa was valid for three months. During the third month my father became very ill and on October 11th he passed away. Both my sisters had to go out to work to help support the family. Sue decided to stay for another three months, if she could get permission from the French government, and we went together to the French embassy to apply for an extension for her visa. I explained that since my father had passed away and my sisters had to go out to work we would like someone to be at home to cook. The extension was granted, which meant that Sue could be in Germany over the Christmas holidays.

Sue's parents were not too happy about their daughter staying for another three months, but said that they understood.

The next few weeks were not the best in Sue's life. However, she made many friends in the village and in the New Apostolic congregation to which we belonged. She also learned the art of German cooking. Food was rationed, but Sue received more than we did because it was calculated on the amount she would be entitled to in England. However, everything went into one pot and was shared equally amongst us. Sue would not have it any other way.

That Christmas was an unforgettable experience for Sue. She loved to hear the carol singers, who went from door to door while the snow was gently falling. This was new to her. There were not many gifts, but the true spirit of Christmas was all the more present. According to tradition, we had managed to get a Christmas tree and light it.

Unknown to me, my sisters arranged for a friend of ours to dress up as Santa Claus with a long beard and come to our house the moment he saw through the window that the Christmas tree lights were being lit.

When there was a knock on the door, I wondered why they asked Sue to open it. To her amazement there was Santa Claus asking if he could come in. He carried a sack full of goodies, given to him by friends and even strangers for Sue and the rest of us. I had never received so many gifts before. Then Santa took off his beard and we recognized him as our dear friend Emil. He was still single at the time so he stayed to join in our own Christmas carol singing. Even though we missed our father and brother, it was one of the nicest Christmases

I could remember.

In February it was time to say good-bye again to my sweetheart Sue. Many in the village were sorry to see her leave.

When she got home, things did not work out too well for Sue. Because she couldn't hide how wonderful everyone had been to her and how nice the German people were, she caused a lot of dissent among her friends and even some relatives. To keep the peace with her parents, she went to stay with one of her aunts, called Aunt Newly, who lived in a nearby village. Her one aim was to save up enough money to return to Germany. We had abandoned the idea of me returning to England. I had a good job and Sue had grown to love the people here. We made plans for marriage.

After returning to England, Sue did not go back to her work as a nurse, but found a job with Sharp Printing, a company which designed and manufactured their own cards, and Sue was one of their artists. That way she was able to earn her air fare more quickly.

In May I received a letter from Sue, telling me that she had booked a one-way flight to Stuttgart for July 22nd. The weeks went by very quickly. Nearly all the village heard that the English girl was going to come back to marry Karl Kern. We found an apartment with a nice family living on the outskirts of the village. A brother of our future landlord owned a pub called Albaufstieg. He offered us the use of his place, free of charge, for the reception.

38

Our wedding was set for September 24th 1950. As was customary in Eningen, a notice was put up in the Town Hall three weeks before that date. Another notice was posted outside the Town Hall in a glass case, so it was visible to any passersby. The notice read: '*Mr. Karl Kern of Eningen and Miss Ursula Ridgway of Clayton, Yorkshire, England are planning to be joined in holy matrimony on the twenty-fourth of September, 1950. If any one should have reason to believe that this marriage should not take place, will they please come forward and say so.*'

Soon everyone in the village knew about the wedding. Invitations went out to our relatives and friends, both in England and Germany. The wedding of the beautiful girl from England was the talk of the village. When the village bakery found out that Ursula's favorite dessert was meringue, topped with fresh blackberries, they offered to make them free for the party, as a gift for the bride. The village butcher, from whom we ordered cold cuts of meat, also supplied them free of charge.

The florist offered to make the table decorations for free. Generally, it was the custom for a bride to carry white roses at her wedding. However Ursula was the first bride in the village to carry pink roses in her bouquet, which started a new trend. On several occasions, when people saw us out walking, they came up to us, put money into our hands and wished us well.

Sue's mother, who was a seamstress, made the wedding dress. It was exquisite, covered in sequins with a beautiful headpiece and a long train.

On a beautiful Sunday morning, Sue was the loveliest bride I had ever seen. We were driven in my brother-in-law's car to a quaint little church on a hillside, surrounded by fields. The bells were ringing and I remembered our engagement by the pond, with the dragonflies dancing, far away in England. My lovely bride waved at the villagers standing by the roadside, waving to us, and the driver of the car was singing *Here comes the bride.*

As we got out of the car and walked towards the church, Sue was looking a little sad. I knew that she was thinking of her family, who could not be present at this special event. I took her by the hand to let her know that I understood. Then I said, "Look Darling." All the small children of the congregation were lined up on both sides of the steps going into the church, holding a small posy of flowers. At the bottom of the steps stood the pageboy, Reinhold, very proud and eager. Sue's face lit up again. The little flower girl was called Brigitte. She looked very pretty in her pink lace dress and threw pink rose petals in our path.

As was the custom, the bride and groom walked together down the aisle to the altar while the organist played a part of Handel's *Largo* that Sue had chosen. It was little Reinhold's duty to carry the bride's veil so it didn't trail on the floor. However, he was so eager that he held the veil up as high as he could, revealing much more of the bride than intended. We were not aware of this until we saw the pictures taken by friends.

After the wedding it was customary for the bride and groom to walk through the streets of the village to the reception. Many villagers lined the streets to see the English bride. Many waved to us out of their windows, wishing us well and throwing money to us. This was picked up by Reinhold and Brigitte, who accompanied us. It seemed as if the whole village took some part in the ceremony.

There were many relatives, friends and guests at the reception. The choir from our little church was there and a small band, including an accordion player and a soloist playing the singing saw. There was no shortage of entertainment. After the reception the now Mr. and Mrs. Kern were driven to their new apartment by the driver who drove us to church.

The next day we went on our honeymoon by train to a small village called Gutenberg, nestling picturesquely in the surrounding woods. We stayed there for four days and then traveled back to our apartment.

A few weeks later we found out that Sue was pregnant with a honeymoon baby. She developed health problems, which made her homesick. Even though everyone was very nice and helpful to her, she began to miss her mother. The doctor's advice was that, for the sake of the baby, we should go back to England.

Much to the dismay of my sisters and all our friends we returned to England and lived in her parents' house. On June 21st the following year our son Peter was born.

We lived in England for fourteen years. In 1964 we emigrated to the United States of America, where we made our home in Wheat Ridge, Colorado.

After a very happy marriage of forty-seven years, my wife Sue passed away on August 31st 1997, which prompted me to write this our incredible love story.

My friend George and I,
in my newly tailored uniform
at the Sawtry POW camp.

Taken in March 1948 on a makeshift theatrical stage
where we put on performances for the British public.

The Kern family

From left to right: Anny, Gertrud, Walter, Luise, myself
In front: My mother Pauline and father Julius

This photo was taken in 1942
before I joined the German Air Force.

The Ridgway family
(without Sue)

(Mother) Dorothy, Pat, Daisy, and (Father) Arthur

Taken in front of their house
at Summer Seat Place, Bradford